To my parents,
Gregg and Sono Harris

Contents

❧

I Gave Josh Harris a Chance

by Sam Torode

I WAS A COLLEGE SENIOR, making a late-night run to Wal-Mart and Taco Bell with my friends. As we walked into Wal-Mart, my eyes were drawn to a book sitting on a rack right inside the door. The cover had a black and white photo of some suave guy—like a young Cary Grant—holding a fedora over his face. I picked it up and started reading the back cover.

"Hey," one of my friends said, "that's the guy all the girls are talking about. The one that says you shouldn't date."

Once, a girl turned me down because I hadn't met her father and gotten his permission to ask her out. *This book must be the source of all the lunacy among girls on our campus,* I decided.

"He doesn't want us to date because he wants all the babes for himself!" I said. "What an arrogant jerk."

Little did I know, at that very moment, five hundred miles away, a beautiful young woman—the sort I hoped to marry some-day—was hanging on every word of *I Kissed Dating Goodbye*. After reading the book, she promised that she would save her first kiss for marriage. A couple years later, she even wrote a magazine article about her decision called "(Don't) Kiss Me."

Somehow, I stumbled onto Bethany's article. Still annoyed that all these young women were being led astray by Josh Harris, I wrote a letter to the editor arguing that not kissing until marriage was just too extreme. (I hadn't kissed anyone before either—but I hoped I wouldn't have to wait many more years.)

Not willing to let me have the last word, the author wrote back to me. One thing led to another, and a few months later, on a cold January day, we met for the first time. I admired Bethany's principled approach to romance—even if I still hated Josh Harris's book (which I'd never actually read).

During a visit with Bethany's family several months later, I found myself alone for an hour and—in a moment of desperate boredom— I pulled her copy of *I Kissed Dating Goodbye* off the shelf and started thumbing through it.

I was expecting to find a long list of rules for "courtship God's way." After a few chapters, I started impatiently skimming ahead. *The rules must be in here somewhere!* To my surprise, I discovered *I Kissed Dating Goodbye* isn't really about dating at all. Instead, it's a book about following Christ and what that means for *all* of our relationships with others—whether romantic or not.

Joshua writes, "Every relationship for a Christian is an opportunity to love another person as God has loved us." That sums up the book's message. Once we embrace this principle, the rest is just details.

Indeed, my own story proves that foregoing casual dating (and even kissing) just might be the thing that brings you and your spouse together. About the time Joshua came out with his second book, *Boy Meets Girl*, Bethany and I shared our first kiss—at the altar.

In the end—in a roundabout way—Josh Harris brought my wife and me together. And now that I've read his books, I admire and recommend them.

Thank you, Josh—my hat's off to you.

Sam Torode

Introduction

THANKS FOR PICKING up this book. Some people never get past the title.

"My friends won't touch it," one girl told me. "They hear the title and say, 'There's no way I would ever do that.'"

One guy urged me to change the title. "More people would read it," he said. Maybe he's right. I heard the story of a confused bookstore customer who asked the owner for a copy of *I Kissed My Date Goodbye*. Now there's a book with a message people would read!

I decided to call this book *I Kissed Dating Goodbye* because I want to be up front with you—there are some radical ideas on these pages. Most other books on dating will tell you how to make dating work for you. This book tells you how to make your life pleasing to God— even if that means taking a break from dating.

So let me make a simple request. Just read the first chapter. If nothing in it grabs you, that's fine. But I think you'll discover that something in this book could help you.

You see, I don't want to argue with you about whether or not you should date. Yes, I'll be honest about the problems I see in the way most people date today. But ultimately my goal isn't to convince you to stop dating. I want to help you examine the aspects of your life that dating touches—the way you treat others, the way you prepare for your future mate, your personal purity—and look at what it means to bring these areas in line with God's Word.

So even though in one sense this book is about dating, in another sense dating isn't *really* the point. The point is what God wants. Discussing if or how to date isn't an end in itself. Talking about it serves a purpose only when we view it in terms of its relation to God's overall plan for our lives.

You may not agree with some of the things I write. That's okay. My hope is that you'll stick around to see what I have to say. If you at least walk away from this book with a little more wisdom, my mission will have been accomplished—and your life could be enhanced. I pray that the ideas shared here will bring you a little closer to God's desire for your life.

So thanks again for picking up the book. Thanks for reading more than the title.

Joshua Harris

PART ONE

Isn't There a Better Way?

CHAPTER ONE

So This Is Love?

Beyond What Feels Good, Back to What *Is* Good

It was finally here—Anna's wedding day, the day she had dreamed about and planned for months. The small, picturesque church was crowded with friends and family.

Sunlight poured through the stained-glass windows, and the gentle music of a string quartet filled the air. Anna walked down the aisle toward David. Joy surged within her. This was the moment for which she had waited so long. He gently took her hand, and they turned toward the altar.

But as the minister began to lead Anna and David through their vows, the unthinkable happened. A girl stood up in the middle of the congregation, walked quietly to the altar, and took David's other hand. Another girl approached and stood next to the first, followed by another. Soon, a chain of six girls stood by him as he repeated his vows to Anna.

Anna felt her lip begin to quiver as tears welled up in her eyes. "Is this some kind of joke?" she whispered to David.

"I'm...I'm sorry, Anna," he said, staring at the floor.

"Who are these girls, David? What is going on?" she gasped.

"They're girls from my past," he answered sadly. "Anna, they don't mean anything to me now…but I've given part of my heart to each of them."

"I thought your heart was mine," she said.

"It is, it is," he pleaded. "Everything that's left is yours."

A tear rolled down Anna's cheek. Then she woke up.

Betrayed

Anna told me about her dream in a letter. "When I awoke I felt so betrayed," she wrote. "But then I was struck with these sickening thoughts: *How many men could line up next to me on my wedding day? How many times have I given my heart away in short-term relationships? Will I have anything left to give my husband?*"

I often think of Anna's dream. The jarring image haunts me. There are girls from my past, too. What if they showed up on my wedding day? What could they say in the receiving line?

"Hello, Joshua. Those were some pretty lofty promises you made at the altar today. I hope you're better at keeping promises now than you were when I knew you."

"My, don't you look nice in that tuxedo. And what a beautiful bride. Does she know about me? Have you told her all the sweet things you used to whisper in *my* ear?"

There are relationships I can only look back on with regret. I do my best to forget. I laugh them off as part of the game of love that everyone plays.

I know that God has been faithful to forgive as I've asked Him to. And I know that the various girls have forgiven me, because I've asked them to.

But I'm still aware of the consequences of my selfishness. I gave my heart away too many times. And I took from girls what wasn't mine.

Living for Myself

My own self-centered approach to romance started young. Even though I grew up in a Christian home, by the time I reached junior high I had embraced a very ungodly attitude toward relationships. I didn't fear God. Despite my parents' diligence and godly example, I was living for sin and my own pleasure.

The older guys on my gymnastics team bragged about the different girls they had slept with. I was mesmerized by their stories. Sin sounded so enticing. With a friend I stole pornographic magazines from a bookstore and pored over them, stoking the fire of my own sinful cravings—I was enslaved to lust, and girls were nothing more than objects to satisfy my desire. One night I snuck out of the house for a prearranged meeting with three girls and made out with each of them one after the other.

Looking back, I'm sickened by these memories, but at the time I only wanted more. The fact that I remained a virgin during those years is, to be honest, a miracle. It had everything to do with God's mercy and nothing to do with any self-control or virtue on my part. I can easily be brought to tears when I think about where I'd be today if God had not chosen to intervene.

God convicted me of my disobedience through a message given by Randy Alcorn at a retreat I attended my freshman year in high school. Randy spoke about heaven. He talked about how Jesus died for my sins. Even though I claimed to be a Christian, as I listened I knew that I wasn't living for God. I had to change.

I repented of my sin right then, and when I got home from the retreat I threw away the pornographic magazines and paid the bookstore for what I'd stolen (I was too embarrassed to tell them in person, but I left a note with the money on the counter). At the same time I quit the gymnastics team and got involved with my church's youth group. My next girlfriend was a Christian and we didn't even kiss. I became a student leader and gained a reputation as someone who was serious about his faith. I assumed that my love life was now pleasing to God.

But I still had a lot to learn.

Not Quite Forever

Although I'm grateful for the changes I made then, I now recognize that much of it was superficial. I wasn't sneaking out to meet girls in the middle of the night anymore, but most of my wrong attitudes remained the same. My main concerns were still my own gratification and the fun I could gain from relationships with girls. I liked the way I felt when a girl liked me. I enjoyed the rush I got from flirting or expressing my feelings to a girl. I was still very immature and selfish.

In church my friends and I played the dating game with passion—more passion, I regret to say, than we gave to worshiping or listening to sermons. During Sunday morning services we passed notes about who liked whom, who was going out with whom, and who had broken up with whom.

During my sophomore year, my involvement in the dating game took a more serious turn. That summer I met Kelly. She had just become a Christian and was new to my church. She was beautiful, blond, and two inches taller than me. But I didn't mind. Kelly was popular, and all the guys liked her. Since I was the only guy who had the nerve to talk to her, she ended up liking me. I asked her to be my girlfriend at the youth group water-ski retreat and sealed our new relationship with a kiss.

Kelly was my first serious girlfriend. Everyone in our youth group recognized us as a couple. We celebrated our "anniversary" every month. Finding ways to spend time together and worrying about the current status of our relationship consumed my energy.

Kelly knew me better than anyone else. After my folks were asleep, Kelly and I would spend hours on the phone, often late into the night, talking about everything and nothing in particular. We thought God had made us for each other. We talked about getting married someday. We began expressing our feelings physically. I promised her that I would love her forever.

My parents didn't want me in a serious relationship, but they adored Kelly. They enjoyed the time she spent with the family. Their love for both of us blinded them to the fact that we were headed in a

dangerous direction. They had no idea about our sinful physical relationship. I hid that from them. I never lied outright to my mom and
dad, but I half-answered questions and tried to put things in a better
light.

Like many high school relationships, our romance was premature—too much, too soon. And our struggle against sexual sin was a
losing battle. Though we never actually had sex, we were dishonoring
God. We were violating each other's purity, and our spiritual lives
were stagnant as a result.

After a summer missions trip that kept us apart for two months, I
ended the relationship.

"We have to break up," I said to her one night after a movie. We
both knew this was coming.

"Is there any chance we can have something in the future?" she
asked.

"No," I said, trying to add resolve to my voice. "No, it's over."

We broke up two years after we'd met. Not quite "forever," as I
had promised.

A Heart Made New

I was seventeen years old when my relationship with Kelly ended. I
walked away asking, "Is this how it's supposed to be?" I felt discouraged, confused, and desperate for an alternative to the cycle of
short-term relationships in which I found myself.

For the first time I really began to question how my faith as a
Christian affected my love life. There had to be more to it than "don't
have sex" and "date only Christians." What did it mean to genuinely
care about the girls I knew? What did it feel like to really be pure—in
my body *and* my heart? And how did God want me to spend my
single years? Was it merely a time to try out different girls romantically? Was dating such a good idea for me?

Books like *Passion and Purity* by Elisabeth Elliot and long talks
with my dad and mom began to change my perspective. Slowly, and
in spite of my resistance, God was peeling away layer after layer of

wrong thinking, wrong values, and wrong desires.

Some people who hear about my decision not to date till I'm ready for marriage assume that my heart must've broken. No, my heart was made new by my Savior. The change in my attitude was the result of realizing the implications of belonging to Him. The Son of God died for me! He came to free me from the hopelessness of living for myself. That *had* to change everything—including my love life. Having a girlfriend was no longer my greatest need. Knowing and obeying Him was. I wanted to please Him in my relationships even if it meant looking radical and foolish to other people—even if it meant kissing dating goodbye.

This Is Love

I've come to understand that God's lordship in my life doesn't merely tinker with my approach to romance—it completely transforms it. God not only wants me to act differently; He wants me to *think* differently—to view love, purity, and singleness from His perspective, to have a new lifestyle and a new attitude.

The basis of this new attitude is God's love for us. John explains the connection between God's love and the way we relate to others in 1 John 4:10–11:

> This is love: not that we loved God, but that he loved us and sent his Son as an atoning sacrifice for our sins. Dear friends, since God so loved us, we also ought to love one another.

Do you see what John is saying? God's amazing love for us at the cross provides both the *example* and the *power* for us to love others. People whose sins have been forgiven through faith in Jesus' death on the cross can't live or love the same ever again. We've been set free from our old self-centered life. We used to be controlled by what felt good, but now, as new creations, we're to be controlled by *God's love*. In 2 Corinthians 5:14–15, Paul writes:

For the love of Christ controls us, because we have concluded this: that one has died for all, therefore all have died;
and he died for all, that those who live might no longer live
for themselves but for him who for their sake died and was
raised. (ESV)

The Bible teaches that if we truly trust in Jesus Christ, we die to
our old way of living. And we can no longer live for ourselves—we
now live for God and for the good of others.

Because of that, relationships with the opposite sex can no longer
be about "having a good time" or "learning what I want in a relationship." They're not to be about getting, but giving. Every relationship
for a Christian is an opportunity to love another person like God has
loved us. To lay down our desires and do what's in his or her best
interest. To care for him or her even when there's nothing in it for us.
To want that person's purity and holiness because it pleases God and
protects him or her.

So whether or not we take a break from dating, if our dating is
controlled by Christ's love it will look so radically different than the
relationships around us that we'll want to come up with a different
name for it!

In recent years, I've tried to let God's love as displayed at the
cross define the way I love members of the opposite sex. This kind of
love leads to some very practical changes in the way a person
approaches relationships. Personally, I've come to some pretty intense
conclusions for my life. I've come to realize that while friendships
with the opposite sex are great, I have no business asking for a girl's
heart and exclusive affections if I'm not ready to consider marriage.
Until I can do that, I'd only be using that girl to meet my short-term
needs, not seeking to bless her for the long term. Would I enjoy having a girlfriend right now? You bet! But I wouldn't truly be loving her
and putting her interests first.

As I've sought God's will for my life, I've discovered that a relationship wouldn't be best for me or for the one I'd date right now.

Instead, by avoiding romantic, one-on-one relationships before God tells me I'm ready, I can better serve girls as a friend, and I can remain free to keep my focus on the Lord.

So even though I'm not romantically attached, I'm loving the girls in my life more than I ever did in the past. And not with the selfish kind of love I practiced so often in the past. I'm loving them based on what *God* says is truly loving.

True love isn't just expressed in passionately whispered words or an intimate kiss or an embrace; before two people are married, love is expressed in self-control, patience, even words left unsaid.

Knowing What's Best

Waiting until I'm ready for commitment before pursuing romance is just one example of letting Christ's love control my relationships with the opposite sex. Each person has to examine his or her own life and ask what it means to love others like Christ. I won't pretend that the day-to-day issues of dealing with attraction or how close a friendship should get are easy to sort through (we'll talk more about this later in the book). But I'm learning to make God's Word, not my feelings, the guide. And as I do, my love is getting smarter. Yes, the Bible actually teaches that our love can and should grow in knowledge. Paul writes in Philippians 1:9–10:

> And this is my prayer: that your love may abound more and more in knowledge and depth of insight, so that you may be able to discern what is best and may be pure and blameless until the day of Christ.

The way we love others should constantly grow and deepen in its knowledge and insight. And when our love grows in knowledge, we can more readily "discern what is best" for our lives. Don't we all desperately need that discernment?

After all, when we engage in guy-girl relationships, we're not always choosing between absolute wrong and absolute right. Often the choice is between what's good and what's best.

For example, even though I decided to quit the dating scene, I don't believe that dating in and of itself is sinful. Because there's no biblical command not to date, this is an area that we each need to evaluate in light of our own maturity, our motive, and the other person involved. The decision requires wisdom.

This is where it's so important that our love for others be shaped by God's love for us. This kind of love looks beyond personal desires and the gratification of the moment. It looks at the big picture: serving others and glorifying God.

"What about me?" you might be asking. "What about *my* needs?" This is the awesome part: When we make God's glory and other people's needs our priority, we position ourselves to receive the greatest joy in our lives as well. Let me explain.

In the past, the starting point of my relationships was what I wanted instead of what God wanted. I looked out for my needs and fit others into my agenda. Did I find fulfillment? No, I found only compromise and heartache. I not only hurt others; I also hurt myself, and most seriously, I sinned against God.

But when I changed my attitude and made pleasing God and blessing others my first priorities, I found true peace and joy. When I stopped seeing girls as potential girlfriends and started treating them as sisters in Christ, I discovered the richness of true friendship. When I stopped worrying about whom I was going to marry and began trusting God's timing, I uncovered the incredible potential of serving God as a single. And when I stopped flirting with temptation in one-on-one dating relationships and started pursuing righteousness, I uncovered the peace and power that come from purity. I kissed dating goodbye because I found out that God has something better in store!

Pure and Blameless

The ultimate goal behind my choice isn't to avoid pain. I'm not afraid of another breakup. I know that even in a godly relationship I might face disappointment one day. No, the reason I want to love like Christ is so that one day I can stand with purity and blamelessness before God. This purity goes beyond sexual purity. While physical purity is very important, God also wants us to pursue purity and blamelessness in our motives, our minds, and our emotions.

Does this mean we'll never sin? Of course not! We can approach God only because of His grace and the sacrifice of His Son, Jesus. And yet this grace doesn't give us license to be lax in our pursuit of righteousness. Instead, it should urge us to desire purity and blamelessness even more.

Ben started dating Alyssa during his senior year of college. For quite some time, he had planned to marry the summer after he graduated. Since he and Alyssa were deeply attracted to each other, he thought she was "the one."

In a letter, Ben told me that he had grown up with high standards in his dating relationships. Alyssa was another story. While Ben had never so much as kissed a girl, kissing was practically a sport for her. Unfortunately, Alyssa's values won out. "When she looked at me with those big brown eyes like I was depriving her of something, I caved," Ben wrote. Their relationship soon became almost entirely physical. They maintained their virginity but only in the technical sense of the word.

A few months later, Alyssa began to be tutored in chemistry by another Christian guy whom Ben had never met. "That was a mistake," Ben wrote angrily. "They were studying chemistry all right—body chemistry!" Alyssa broke up with Ben and the next day was hanging on the arm of her new boyfriend.

"I was crushed," Ben told me. "I had violated my own standards, and more important, God's standards, and it turned out that this wasn't the woman I was to marry." For several months Ben wrestled with guilt but finally laid it at the foot of the cross and moved on, determined not to make the same mistake twice. But what about Alyssa? Yes, God can forgive her, too. But I wonder if she has ever realized she needs that forgiveness. When she passes Ben at school or sees him in the cafeteria, what goes through her mind? Does she realize she played a part in tearing down his purity? Does she feel pangs of guilt for breaking his heart? Does she even care?

I believe the time has come for Christians, male and female, to own up to the mess we've left behind in our selfish pursuit of short-term romance. What excuse will we have when God asks us to account for our actions and attitudes in relationships? If God sees a sparrow fall (Matthew 10:29), do you think He could possibly over-look the broken hearts and hurt we cause in relationships based on selfishness?

Everyone around us may be doing it. But at the end of our lives, we won't answer to everyone. We'll answer to God. Our actions in relationships haven't escaped God's notice. But here's the good news: The God who sees all our sin is ready to forgive if we repent and turn from them.

Because of Jesus' sacrifice for me, I know that God has forgiven me for the sins I've committed against Him and against the girlfriends I've had. I don't have to live overwhelmed by regret or fear of the future. Because we serve a God who makes all things new, the wedding nightmare my friend Anna had doesn't have to be ours—no matter how many mistakes we've made in the past.

It's this grace, this mercy, that should motivate us to live differently for the rest of our lives.

I'm an unworthy sinner that God chose to rescue and forgive.

This is love.

And because I've experienced it—because Jesus died for me—I'm committed to a love life that's controlled by Him. I invite you along. In light of the love He's given us, let's make purity and blame-lessness our priority.

CHAPTER TWO

The Little Relationship Principle

(That Leads to Big Change)

The Joy of Intimacy Is the Reward of Commitment

IT WAS THREE MINUTES till the show started. From backstage I could hear the studio audience clapping. A production assistant wearing a headset guided me to a small room right off the set. "Wait here until I call you," he said and then disappeared.

Already seated in the cramped space was a fellow guest for the show, an actor named Ben Affleck. He was watching the host's opening monologue on a small television.

"How you doin'?" he asked as I sat down next to him.

"Okay, I guess," I said. "But I've never really done anything like this, so I'm a little nervous."

He nodded. "I still get nervous even though I've done so many. So you're doin' alright."

The guy with the headset stuck his head in the room. "Okay, c'mon. You're on in thirty seconds."

Anti-Dating Activist

The late-night television show was called *Politically Incorrect*. The host was Bill Maher, an irreverent and sharp-tongued former stand-up comic. Each night he and an eclectic panel of guests would sit around and discuss politics and other current issues.

The guests who appeared on the show fell into predictable categories: actors, politicians, rock stars, comedians, and extremists with weird ideas. Being the author of a book titled *I Kissed Dating Goodbye* put me in the last group.

Because of the show's fast pace and sarcastic tone, I knew I'd have trouble getting my message across, but it was even harder than I expected. I cringed when I walked onto the set and the announcer introduced me as an "anti-dating activist."

My fellow guests that night were Steven Wright, a comedian known for his deadpan humor; Christine O'Donnell, a media-savvy fellow Christian who had been on the show fourteen times; and Ben Affleck, an actor whose good looks and rising stardom were the sole reason thousands of teenage girls would be tuning in.

The cameras rolled. *God, please don't let me say anything really dumb.* Bill Maher looked at me. "Let's talk a little bit about your book," he said holding it up. "It's very provocative, very interesting. Basically your thesis is that the best way to find the person of your dreams is to stop dating."

Before I could answer, Ben Affleck interrupted. "How are you going to find the person of your dreams if you stop dating?"

"Well, it's not quite as simple as just 'not dating,'" I said. "The idea is that a lot of the things we do in relationships today are motivated by selfishness. We're starting what we can't finish, we're pursuing romance when we're really not interested in commitment. And so what I'm challenging people to do is rethink their whole approach to relationships and wait until they're…"

"Why does commitment have to be the goal?" Bill interrupted.

"What are the other options?" I asked. "If it's not commitment, is it just for the heck of it?"

"That's selfish," Christine O'Donnell said in my defense.

"No, it's just giving it a shot," Ben said with a smirk. "You know what I mean?" The audience clapped approvingly.

"Why is it you Christians always want the rest of us to do things *your* way?" Bill asked in an irritated tone. "What about a man and a woman, neither of whom wants commitment? What if both of them are just out for fun?"

What's Really the Point?

How would you answer Bill's question? Many relationships today are exactly like the ones he describes: two people out for a good time with no interest in anything more. Is that a problem? Does commitment need to be the goal of a romantic relationship?

The answer you give is very important. I believe that the fundamental problem with relationships today is that we've disconnected romance and commitment.

Jayme was a junior in high school; her boyfriend, Troy, was a senior. Troy was everything Jayme ever wanted in a guy, and for eight months they were inseparable. But two months before Troy left for college, he abruptly announced that he didn't want to see Jayme anymore.

"When we broke up it was definitely the toughest thing that's ever happened to me," Jayme told me afterward. Even though physically they'd never gone beyond a kiss, Jayme had completely given her heart and emotions to Troy. Troy had enjoyed the intimacy while it served his needs but then rejected her when he was ready to move on.

Does Jayme's story sound familiar to you? Perhaps you've heard something similar from a friend, or maybe you've experienced it yourself. Like many relationships, Jayme and Troy's became intimate with little or no thought about commitment or how either of them would be affected when it ended. We can blame Troy for being a jerk, but let's ask ourselves a question: What's really the point of most dating relationships? Often we're pursuing intimacy for the sake of intimacy—two people getting close to each other without any real intention of making a long-term commitment.

But think about this. Deepening intimacy without defining a level of commitment is dangerous. It's like going mountain climbing with a partner who isn't sure she wants the responsibility of holding your rope. When you've climbed two thousand feet up a mountain face, you don't want to have a conversation about how she feels "tied down" by your relationship. In the same way, many people experience deep hurt when they open themselves up emotionally and physically only to be abandoned by someone who proclaims he's not ready for a "serious commitment."

A Little Principle

An intimate relationship is a beautiful experience that God wants us to enjoy. After all, He stated that it wasn't good for man to be alone and created the woman to perfectly complement him and help him (Genesis 2:18). But God has made the fulfillment of intimacy a by-product of commitment-based love. If we want to experience the goodness of His plan, we need to reconnect the pursuit of intimacy with the pursuit of commitment. This is what I call the Little Relationship Principle:

> *The joy of intimacy is the reward of commitment.*

All of us want intimacy. It means being close to someone. It's being vulnerable, open, and dependent. It's giving to and receiving from another person the deepest parts of who we are—our hopes, our fears, our secrets, our affections. An intimate relationship in which we know and are known by another human is one of the most fulfilling and precious parts of life—it's a gift from God.

There are many different kinds of intimate relationships in life. We can be intimate with a friend, with a family member, with a coworker, but the deepest, most meaningful of intimate relationships (outside of a Christian's relationship with God) is the one between a husband and wife who share not only their hearts but also their bodies—in sexual intimacy, two people know each other in a profound way.

What each of these relationships has in common is trust. We are intimate with those people who have proven their faithfulness to us, people who have shown over time that they will be careful to guard what we have given of ourselves. We're intimate with people who are committed to us.

You might say that intimacy between a man and a woman is the icing on the cake of a relationship headed toward marriage. And if we look at intimacy that way, then it becomes obvious that most of our dating relationships are all icing. They usually lack a purpose or a clear destination. In most cases, especially when we're younger, dating is short term, serving the needs of the moment. We date because we want to enjoy the emotional and physical benefits of intimacy without the responsibility of real commitment.

Front Porch to Backseat

This is what the whole revolution of dating was all about. It's helpful to understand that the concept of "dating" is a relatively recent idea. It hasn't been around forever. As I see it, dating is a product of our entertainment-driven, disposable-everything American culture.

At the turn of the twentieth century, the connection between intimacy and commitment was much stronger than it is today. Usually a guy and girl became romantically involved only if they planned to marry. If a young man spent time at a girl's home, family and friends assumed that he intended to propose to her. But shifting attitudes in culture and the arrival of the automobile brought radical changes. The new "rules" allowed people to indulge in all the thrills of romantic love without having any intention of marriage. Author Beth Bailey documents these changes in a book whose title, *From Front Porch to Backseat*, says everything about the difference in society's attitude when dating became the norm. Intimacy didn't have to be accompanied by deepening obligation or responsibility to another person.

Love and romance became things people could enjoy solely for their recreational value.

Since the 1920s, intimacy and commitment have only been further separated. In her book *A Return to Modesty,* secular author Wendy Shalit documents how our generation has made sexual intimacy an end in itself. Commitment is a thing of the past. What we have instead, Shalit says, is the *hook-up*. She explains:

> Hook-up is my generation's word for having sex (or oral sex) or sometimes for what used to be called "making out." The hook-up connotes the most casual of connections.... In context, the typical exchange is, "I hooked up last night." "Yeah? Me, too." Above all, it is *no big deal*. Indeed, hooking up is so casual, and the partners so interchangeable, that sometimes it's hard to discern a pattern in all the hooking and unhooking. It seems almost arbitrary.

The hook-up is the ultimate expression of intimacy *devoid of* commitment—two people who are out for a good time and want the pleasure of an intimate sexual encounter without any of the responsibility of a relationship. Ironically, Shalit points out that for many singles even the most casual of dating relationships is more obligation than they care to shoulder. They're "kissing dating goodbye" but for all the *wrong* reasons. Instead of not dating because they're waiting to pursue a committed relationship, they're not dating because dating itself is *too much* commitment.

Good, Clean, Christian Hook-Ups

Christians agree that sexual intimacy outside of the lifelong commitment of marriage is sinful. But while we frown on the idea of sexual hook-ups, we have our own "sanitized" Christian version of the hook-up in recreational dating.

The truth is, we've bought into our culture's self-centered mindset.

We haven't carried our assumptions to their logical conclusion like our secular neighbors have, but we have the same wrong assumptions they do. We're only a few steps behind on the same path. We pursue romantic relationships for the sake of romance, for a good time, for the sake of the experience, for the sake of figuring out what we'll one day want when we get around to actually committing to one person.

As I shared in the previous chapter, my own life is an example of this flawed thinking. Even when I stopped pursuing blatant sexual sin, I still had the hook-up mentality—I'd merely traded physical hook-ups for emotional ones. I wanted to be able to enjoy romance before marriage, to become intimate and close with whomever I wanted—commitment wasn't even a consideration.

Love and Faithfulness

What we fail to see is that the intimacy we experience in our string of emotional hook-ups is counterfeit. Romantic passion is sweetest when it's growing out of a relationship that's deepening in devotion.

The joy of intimacy is the reward of commitment.

Throughout the Bible we see that the Little Relationship Principle is an important aspect of true love. In the Old Testament, God makes a covenant—a binding commitment—with the people of Israel so that they can know Him intimately. The institution of marriage is founded on the same principle. A man and woman become one flesh and enjoy the deepest intimacy with each other only after they've made a public promise to love each other for life.

Proverbs 3:3 states, "Let love and faithfulness never leave you; bind them around your neck, write them on the tablet of your heart." God wants love and faithfulness to be connected. In His plan, the personal benefits of an intimate relationship—emotional or sexual—are always closely linked to self-sacrificial love and commitment to another person's long-term good.

The way of sin is to try to divorce the two. In Proverbs 7 we read of the seductress, who lures her victim with the offer of romantic and sexual pleasures devoid of responsibility. "Come, let's drink deep of love till morning; let's enjoy ourselves with love!" (v. 18). This is how sin works. It calls us to "enjoy ourselves with love" without worrying about the good of others. It offers intimacy without obligation.

Pursuing intimacy without commitment awakens desires—emotional and physical—that neither person can justly meet. In 1 Thessalonians 4:6 (KJV) the Bible calls this "defrauding," ripping someone off by raising expectations but not delivering on the promise. Pastor Stephen Olford describes defrauding as "arousing a hunger we cannot righteously satisfy"—promising something we cannot or will not provide.

Intimacy without commitment, like icing without cake, can be sweet, but it ends up making us sick.

Applying the Principle

As you can see, intimacy without commitment contradicts what the Bible teaches about true love. Instead of being selfless, it's selfish; instead of being patient, it's impatient; instead of looking out for the ongoing good of the other person, it's focused on the needs of the moment.

And this is why remembering that *intimacy is the reward of commitment* is so important. This little principle is a practical way to practice the Golden Rule in romance—it's deciding to do what's best for others by never asking for intimacy that you're not able to match with commitment.

This is the reason I stopped dating. Not because I don't want to get married. Not because I don't enjoy romance. But because I realized that I need to wait on romance until I can match my pursuit of intimacy with a pursuit of commitment.

It doesn't mean I have no relationships with the opposite sex or no intimacy, but rather *appropriate* relationships and *appropriate* intimacy. I pursue friendships with girls. These relationships are dynamic and enriching.

As Christians we should never neglect or ignore our relationships with the opposite sex. Do you know why? Because God tells us that as Christians we have a built-in level of commitment to each other as "brothers and sisters" in Christ (1 Timothy 5:1–2). We're family. And while there are limits to how close men and women can be in friendships, we can't shirk our responsibility to care for, encourage, and build up our brothers and sisters.

But how close can we get before the relationship has to be redefined? How far can we go as friends before our hearts kick into gear? The little relationship principle helps us sort through these difficult questions. We don't ask for a level of intimacy and emotional loyalty that goes beyond our true level of commitment. If we're not able to deepen in commitment and pursue the possibility of marriage, we should halt the progression of intimacy at the friendship stage.

What I hope you understand is that this concept transcends the issue of whether you're officially "dating" someone. Obviously, going on dates and placing yourself in romantically charged settings with someone will usually accelerate the intimacy of your relationship. But you don't have to go out on a date to become inappropriately intimate. You can do that over the phone, via e-mail, or on group dates. A guy and a girl meeting over lunch isn't the issue. The issue is whether the intimacy in your relationship is appropriate to your current level of commitment.

Careful What You Wish For

The best relationships are between two people who care more about each other's good than their own momentary pleasure. The Little Relationship Principle won't make romance risk-free or foolproof. But it can guide and direct us toward healthy, God-pleasing relationships. And it can help us obey the second great command to love others as we love ourselves (Matthew 22:39).

But what about the fun we miss out on by waiting to match romance with commitment? I don't think we miss much. The pleasure of our hook-ups is fleeting.

When I was on *Politically Incorrect*, the host asked me why commitment has to be the goal. "What if both of them are just out for fun?"

"That's the way a lot of relationships work," I admitted. "And I know they're not going to stop just because I wrote a book. But what I hope to show them is the beauty of pursuing a relationship that *is* based on commitment. Because a lot of people live like that and they come to the end of their life, and they find their life is empty."

Have you experienced that emptiness in your relationships? Are you willing to reconsider the connection between intimacy and commitment? Maybe what we call "giving a relationship a shot" without thought to commitment is really selfishness. Maybe the harmless fun we've pursued in recreational romance isn't so harmless after all.

I was sad to read not long ago that Ben Affleck had admitted himself to a rehab clinic for alcohol abuse. The article quoted his friends as saying that his heavy drinking started when a famous actress he'd been seeing ended their relationship. Drinking was his way of trying to drown out the pain. I guess even actors get their hearts broken.

I remember something he said moments before the show started. I asked him how it felt to win an Oscar, to be famous and have his career take off.

"Is this what you always dreamed of?" I asked.

"Yeah, I guess it is," Ben replied. But it comes with a price, he told me. Becoming a star changed his relationships; it strained old ties. "I guess you have to be careful what you wish for," he concluded.

And I think that's the story of our generation's pursuit of fulfillment in relationships. We wished for intimacy without obligation. We wished for sex with no strings attached. We wished for the pleasure of love with none of the work, none of the vows, none of the sacrifice.

And we got it.

But the results aren't what we hoped for. And we're left feeling emptier than before. The intimacy is superficial. The sex leaves us dissatisfied and hungry for something real, something true.

Where is true joy? It's found in God's brand of love—love founded on faithfulness, love rooted in commitment.

The joy of intimacy is the reward of commitment.

⤳

CHAPTER THREE

The Seven Habits of Highly Defective Dating

Recognizing Dating's Negative Tendencies

W HEN I WAS A KID, my mom taught me two rules of grocery shopping. First, never shop when you're hungry—everything will look good and you'll spend too much money. And second, make sure to pick a good cart.

I've got the first rule down, but I haven't had much success with that second rule. I seem to have a knack for picking rusty grocery carts that make clattering noises or ones with squeaky wheels that grate on your nerves like fingernails on a chalkboard.

But by far the worst kind of cart you could pick is the "swerver." Have you ever dealt with one of these? This kind of cart has a mind of its own. You want to go in a straight line, but the cart wants to swerve to the left and take out the cat food display. (And much to your dismay and embarrassment, it often succeeds!) The shopper who has chosen a swerving cart can have no peace. Every maneuver, from turning down the cereal aisle to gliding alongside the meat section, becomes a battle—the shopper's will pitted against the cart's.

Why am I talking to you about shopping carts when this book is about relationships? Well, I recall my bad luck with grocery carts because many times I've experienced a similar battle of wills with dating. I'm not talking about conflicts between me and the girls I've dated. I'm talking about the struggle I've had with the whole system. And based on my experiences and my exploration of God's Word, I've concluded that for Christians typical dating can often be a swerver—an approach to relationships that wants to go in a different direction than the one God has for us.

Part of the Problem

As we saw in the first two chapters, dating in and of itself isn't the cause of the problems we see in relationships. Sinful and selfish *people* are the cause of sinful and selfish *relationships*—it's our own wrong attitudes and values that make for defective dating.

But while dating isn't necessarily wrong, we've got to keep in mind that the system of dating as we know it grew out of a culture that celebrates self-centeredness and immorality. Just as a bar that sells alcohol doesn't force anyone to drink and isn't the cause of drunkenness, a bar is an establishment created so that people can have a place to drink and get drunk. You wouldn't say that getting rid of bars would end alcoholism or that everyone who visits a bar has a drinking problem, but neither would you encourage a friend who was trying to quit drinking to hang out in bars. The setting of a bar would only facilitate his likeliness to succumb to his temptation.

In a similar way, the system of dating can encourage the sinful desires of our hearts. No, dating doesn't make us sin. And no, getting rid of it wouldn't solve all our problems in relationships. But it would be foolish to pretend that dating itself isn't at least part of the problem.

Self-Control Isn't Enough

I once heard a youth minister speak on the topic of love and sex. He told a heart-rending story about Ben and Lisa, two strong Christians who had actively participated in his youth group years earlier. Ben and Lisa's dating relationship had started out innocently—Friday nights at the movies and rounds of putt-putt golf. But as time went by, their physical relationship slowly began to accelerate, and they ended up sleeping together. Soon afterward they broke up, discouraged and hurt.

The pastor saw both of them years later at a high school reunion. Lisa was now married and had a child. Ben was still single. But both came to him separately and expressed emotional trauma and guilt over past memories.

"When I see him, I remember it all so vividly," Lisa cried.

Ben expressed similar feelings. "When I see her, the hurt comes back," he told his former youth pastor. "The wounds still haven't healed."

When the youth minister had finished telling this story, you could have heard a pin drop. We all sat waiting for some sort of resolution. We knew the reality of the story he told. Some of us had made the same mistake or watched it happen in the lives of our friends. We wanted something better. We wanted the pastor to tell us what we were supposed to do instead.

But he gave no alternative that afternoon. Evidently the pastor thought the couple's *only* mistake was giving in to temptation. He seemed to think that Ben and Lisa only needed to have more respect for each other and more self-control. Although this pastor encouraged a different outcome—saving sex for marriage—he didn't offer a different practice.

Is this the answer? Head out on the same course with the same assumptions and attitudes as those who have fallen and hope that in the critical moment you'll be able to stay in control? Giving people this kind of advice is like sending a person with a cart that swerves into a store stocked with the world's most expensive Chinaware. This person is expected to navigate narrow aisles between shelves laden with delicate dishes while steering a cart known to go off course? I don't think so.

Yet this is exactly what we try in many of our relationships. We see the failed attempts around us, but we refuse to replace the "cart" of this world's approach to dating. We want to stay on the straight and narrow path and serve God, yet we continue a practice that often pulls us in the wrong direction.

Defective Dating

The majority of this book addresses our attitudes and the issues of the heart that affect how we relate to others. But in this chapter I want to examine what I consider problems with the dating system itself. Whether or not you choose to take a break from dating, I think this will help you steer clear of defective relationships.

If we continue to date according to the system as it exists today, we'll more than likely swerve into trouble. Good intentions aren't enough. Ben and Lisa probably had good intentions, but like many Christian couples today they founded their relationship on our culture's defective attitudes and patterns for romance. Unfortunately, even in their adulthood they continue to reap the consequences.

The following seven habits of highly defective dating are some of the "swerves" dating relationships often make. Perhaps you can relate to one or two of them. (I know I can!)

1. DATING TENDS TO SKIP THE FRIENDSHIP STAGE OF A RELATIONSHIP.

Jack met Libby at a church-sponsored college retreat. Libby was a friendly girl with a reputation for taking her relationship with God seriously. Jack and Libby chatted during a game of volleyball and seemed to really hit it off. Jack wasn't interested in an intense relationship, but he wanted to get to know Libby better. Two days after the retreat he called her up and asked if she'd like to go out to a movie the next weekend. She said yes.

Did Jack make the right move? Well, he did in terms of scoring a date, but if he really wanted to build a friendship, he more than likely struck out. One-on-one dating has the tendency to move a guy and girl beyond friendship and toward romance too quickly.

Have you ever known someone who worried about dating a

longtime friend? If you have, you probably heard that person say something like this: "He asked me out, but I'm just afraid that if we start actually *dating* it will change our friendship." What is this person really saying? People who make statements like that, whether they realize it or not, recognize that dating encourages romantic expectations. In a true friendship you don't feel pressured by knowing that you "like" the other person or that he or she "likes" you back. You feel free to be yourself and do things together without spending three hours in front of the mirror making sure you look perfect.

C. S. Lewis describes friendship as two people walking side by side toward a common goal. Their mutual interest brings them together. Jack skipped this commonality stage by asking Libby out on a typical, no-brainer, dinner-and-movie date where their "coupleness" was the focus.

In dating, romantic attraction is often the cornerstone of the relationship. The premise of dating is "I'm attracted to you; therefore, let's get to know each other." The premise of friendship, on the other hand, is "We're interested in the same things; let's enjoy these common interests together." If romantic attraction forms after developing a friendship, it's an added bonus.

Intimacy without commitment is defrauding. Intimacy without friendship is superficial. A relationship based solely on physical attraction and romantic feelings will last only as long as the feelings last.

2. DATING OFTEN MISTAKES A PHYSICAL RELATIONSHIP FOR LOVE.

Dave and Heidi didn't mean to make out with each other on their first date. Really. Dave doesn't have "only one thing on his mind," and Heidi isn't "that kind of girl." It just happened. They had gone to a concert together and afterward watched a video at Heidi's house. During the movie, Heidi made a joke about Dave's attempt at dancing during the concert. He started tickling her. Their playful wrestling suddenly stopped when they found themselves staring into each other's eyes as Dave was leaning over her on the living room floor.

They kissed. It was like something out of a movie. It felt so right.

It may have felt right, but the early introduction of physical affection into their relationship added confusion. Dave and Heidi hadn't really gotten to know each other, but suddenly they felt close. As the relationship progressed, they found it difficult to remain objective. Whenever they would try to evaluate the merits of their relationship, they'd immediately picture the intimacy and passion of their physical relationship. *It's so obvious we love each other,* Heidi thought. But did they? Just because lips have met doesn't mean hearts have joined. And just because two bodies are drawn to each other doesn't mean two people are right for each other. A physical relationship doesn't equal love.

When we consider that our culture as a whole regards the words *love* and *sex* as interchangeable, we shouldn't be surprised that many dating relationships mistake physical attraction and sexual intimacy for true love. Sadly, many Christian dating relationships reflect this false mindset.

When we examine the progression of most relationships, we can clearly see how dating can encourage this substitution. First, as we pointed out in chapter two, most often dating isn't a pursuit of commitment. For this reason, many dating relationships begin with physical attraction. The underlying attitude is that a person's primary value comes from the way he or she looks. Even before a kiss has been given, the physical, sensual aspect of the relationship has taken priority.

Next, the relationship often steamrolls toward intimacy. Because dating doesn't require commitment, the two people involved allow the needs and passions of the moment to take center stage. The couple doesn't look at each other as possible life partners or weigh the responsibilities of marriage. Instead, they focus on the demands of the present. And with that mindset, the couple's physical relationship can easily become the focus.

Sadly, many couples gauge the seriousness of their relationship by the level of their physical involvement. Two people who date each other want to feel that they're special to each other, and they can concretely express this through physical intimacy. They begin to distinguish their special relationship through hand-holding, kissing, and everything else that follows. For this reason, many people believe that going out with someone means physical involvement.

Focusing on the physical is plainly sinful. God demands sexual purity. And He does this because He is holy. He also does it for our own good. Physical involvement can distort two people's perspective of each other and lead to unwise choices. God also knows we'll carry the memories of our past physical involvements into marriage. He doesn't want us to live with guilt and regret.

Physical involvement can make two people feel close. But if many people really examined the focus of their dating relationships, they'd probably discover that all they have in common is lust.

3. DATING OFTEN ISOLATES A COUPLE FROM OTHER VITAL RELATIONSHIPS.

While Garreth and Jenny were dating, they didn't need anyone else. Since it meant spending time with Jenny, Garreth had no problem giving up Wednesday night Bible study with the guys. Jenny didn't think twice about how little she talked to her younger sister and mother now that she was dating Garreth. Nor did she realize that when she did talk to them, she was always saying something like "Garreth this…" and "Garreth said such and such…" Without intending to, both had foolishly and selfishly cut themselves off from other relationships.

By its very definition, dating is about two people focusing on each other. Unfortunately, in most cases the rest of the world fades into the background. If you've ever felt like a third wheel when hanging out with two friends who are dating each other, you know how true this is.

Now, in a relationship where both people are prepared to move toward marriage, giving the relationship primary attention is not wrong. To make a wise choice about marrying someone, it's important to focus on getting to know that person well. But even in serious relationships it's not wise to isolate yourself from others.

For people who really aren't ready for commitment, this dating tendency can be especially detrimental. Christians need to take this seriously. Why? First, because when we allow one relationship to crowd out others, we lose perspective. In Proverbs 15:22 we read, "Plans fail for lack of counsel, but with many advisers they succeed." If we make our decisions about life based solely on the influence of one relationship, we'll probably make poor judgments.

Of course we can make this same mistake in any number of non-romantic relationships. But we face this problem more often in dating relationships because these relationships involve our hearts and emotions. And because dating focuses on the plans of a couple, major issues related to marriage, family, and faith are likely at stake.

And if two people haven't defined their level of commitment, they're particularly at risk. You put yourself in a precarious position if you isolate yourself from the people who love and support you because you dive wholeheartedly into a romantic relationship not grounded in commitment. In *Passion and Purity,* Elisabeth Elliot states, "Unless a man is prepared to ask a woman to be his wife, what right has he to claim her exclusive attention? Unless she has been asked to marry him, why would a sensible woman promise any man her exclusive attention?" How many people end dating relationships only to find their ties to other friends severed?

When Garreth and Jenny mutually decided to stop dating, they were surprised to find their other friendships in disrepair. It's not that their other friends didn't like them; it's just that they hardly knew Garreth and Jenny anymore. Neither had invested any time or effort in maintaining these friendships while they concentrated on their dating relationship.

Perhaps you've done a similar thing. Or maybe you know the pain and frustration of being put on the back burner for the sake of a friend's boyfriend or girlfriend. The exclusive attention so often expected in dating relationships has a tendency to isolate them from the friends who love them most, family members who know them best, and sadly, even God, whose will is far more important than any romantic interest.

4. DATING CAN DISTRACT YOUNG ADULTS FROM THEIR PRIMARY RESPONSIBILITY OF PREPARING FOR THE FUTURE.

We cannot live in the future, but neglecting our current obligations will disqualify us for tomorrow's responsibilities. Being distracted by love is not such a bad thing—unless God wants you doing something else.

One of the saddest tendencies of dating is to distract young adults from developing their God-given abilities and skills. Instead of serving in their local church, instead of equipping themselves with the character, education, and experience necessary to succeed in life, many allow themselves to be consumed by the present needs that dating emphasizes.

Christopher and Stephanie started dating when they were both fifteen years old. In many ways, they had the model dating relationship. They never got involved physically, and when they broke up two years later, their breakup was amicable. So what harm was done? Well, none in the sense that they didn't get into trouble. But we can begin to see some problems when we look at what Christopher and Stephanie could have been doing instead. Maintaining a relationship takes a lot of time and energy. Christopher and Stephanie spent countless hours talking, writing, thinking, and often worrying about their relationship. The energy they exerted stole from other pursuits. For Christopher, the relationship drained his enthusiasm for his hobby of computer programming and his involvement with the church's worship band. Though Stephanie doesn't hold it against Christopher, she rejected several opportunities to go on short-term missions because she didn't want to be away from him. Their relationship swallowed up time both of them could have spent developing skills and exploring new opportunities.

Dating may help you practice being a good boyfriend or girlfriend, but are these the skills we need for marriage? Even if you're going out with the person you will one day marry, a preoccupation with being the perfect boyfriend or girlfriend now can actually hinder you from being the future husband or wife that person will one day need.

5. DATING CAN CAUSE DISCONTENTMENT WITH GOD'S GIFT OF SINGLENESS.

On my brother's third birthday, he received a beautiful blue bicycle. The miniature bike was brand-new, complete with training wheels, protective padding, and streamers. I thought he couldn't ask for a better first bike, and I couldn't wait to see his reaction.

But to my chagrin my brother didn't seem impressed with the present. When my dad pulled the bike out of its large cardboard box, my brother looked at it a moment, smiled, then began playing with the box. It took my family and me a few days to convince him that the real gift was the bike.

I can't help but think that God views our infatuation with short-term dating relationships much as I did my brother's love for a worthless box. A string of uncommitted dating relationships is not the gift! God gives us singleness—a season of our lives unmatched in its boundless opportunities for growth, learning, and service—and we view it as a chance to get bogged down in finding and keeping boyfriends and girlfriends. But we don't find the real beauty of singleness in pursuing romance with as many different people as we want. We find the real beauty in using our freedom to serve God with abandon.

Recreational dating causes dissatisfaction because it encourages a wrong use of this freedom. God has placed a desire in most men and women for marriage. Although we don't sin when we look forward to marriage, we might be guilty of poor stewardship of our singleness when we allow a desire for something God obviously doesn't have for us *yet* to rob our ability to enjoy and appreciate what He *has* given us. Dating plays a role in fostering this dissatisfaction because it gives single people just enough intimacy to make them wish they had more. Instead of enjoying the unique qualities of singleness, dating causes people to focus on what they don't have.

6. DATING CAN CREATE AN ARTIFICIAL ENVIRONMENT FOR EVALUATING ANOTHER PERSON'S CHARACTER.

Although most dating relationships don't head toward marriage, some—especially those among older singles—are motivated by marriage. People who sincerely want to find out if someone is potential marriage material need to understand that typical dating actually hinders that process. Dating creates an artificial environment for two people to interact in. As a result, each person can easily convey an equally artificial image.

In the driveway of our house we have a basketball hoop that we can adjust to different heights. When I lower the hoop three feet from its normal setting, I can look like a pretty good basketball player. Dunking is no problem. I glide across the pavement and slam the ball down every time. But my "skill" exists only because I've lowered the standards—I'm not playing in a real environment. Put me on a court with a ten-foot hoop, and I'm back to being a short guy who can't jump.

In a similar way, dating creates an artificial environment that doesn't require a person to accurately portray his or her positive and negative characteristics. On a date, a person can charm his or her way into a date's heart. He drives a nice car and pays for everything; she looks great. But who cares? Being fun on a date doesn't say anything about a person's character or ability to be a good husband or wife.

Part of the reason dating is fun is that it gives us a break from real life. For this reason, when I'm married I plan to make a habit of dating my wife. In marriage, you need to take breaks from the stress of kids and work; you *need* to just get away for a bit. But two people weighing the possibility of marriage need to make sure they don't interact only within the fun, romantic settings of dating. Their priority shouldn't be to get away from real life; they need a strong dose of objective reality! They need to see each other in the real-life settings of family and friends. They need to watch each other serving and working. How does he interact with the people who know him best? How does she react when things don't go perfectly? When considering a potential mate, we need to find the answers to these kinds of questions—questions that dating won't answer.

7. DATING OFTEN BECOMES AN END IN ITSELF.

I once talked to Marty, a guy in his midtwenties who enthusiastically told me about his girlfriend, Claire. They'd been dating for four years. She was a wonderful girl, he said, and they had a terrific relationship.

I assumed since they'd been together so long that engagement must be on the horizon and asked, "When do you think you guys will get married?"

Marty was shocked that I'd even mentioned marriage and began to vigorously backpedal. "Well, gosh, we're just dating," he stammered. "That doesn't mean…well, I don't know if I want to marry her."

I wouldn't encourage anyone to marry someone just because they'd dated a long time. But I wondered what Marty needed to learn about Claire after four years together that would help him decide. I suspect that, like many relationships today, Marty and Claire were stuck in what I call "dating limbo." Instead of acting as a bridge between friendship and marriage, dating becomes the destination— not ending but not moving on, either.

Singles who grow accustomed to dating limbo often find it difficult to leave. It's so comfortable! Because they can experience many of the emotional and, sadly, even physical privileges of marriage in their dating relationships, many people (men in particular) find little motivation for committing themselves to marriage.

For the man or woman who is ready to get married, the dating scene and the habits it encourages aren't helpful. It can seem like you're making something happen but you might just be getting into a holding pattern of one short-term relationship after another.

Old Habits Die Hard

Do you see any of these habits in your own life? While not all dating relationships make all these mistakes, what I hope you see is that the problems in dating can't all be fixed by merely "dating right." I believe that dating has tendencies to swerve that don't go away just because Christians do the steering. And even those Christians who can avoid the major pitfalls of premarital sex and traumatic breakups often spend much of their energy wrestling with temptation.

If you've dated, this probably sounds familiar to you. I think that for too long we've approached relationships using the world's mindset and values, and if you've tried it, you might agree with me that it just doesn't work. Let's not waste any more time wrestling with the swerving cart of dating. It's time for a new attitude.

CHAPTER FOUR

Counterculture Romance

Five Attitude Changes to Help
You Avoid Defective Dating

IN THE PREVIOUS CHAPTER, I outlined the seven habits of highly defective dating. Perhaps that chapter challenged the way you think about dating. If so, you're probably saying to yourself, "I can agree that dating has its problems. But what do I do now? *How* do Christians avoid defective dating?"

The first step is to change your attitude toward relationships. Easier said than done, right? But in Ephesians 4:22–24 (NLT), Paul reminds us that through faith in Christ, God has made us new people who can leave behind old ways of living:

> Throw off your old evil nature and your former way of life, which is rotten through and through, full of lust and deception. Instead, there must be a spiritual renewal of your thoughts and attitudes. You must display a new nature because you are a new person, created in God's likeness— righteous, holy, and true.

Until we renew our ways of thinking about love and relationships, our lifestyles will continue to flounder in the mire of defective
dating.

In this chapter, I'd like to clearly state the perspective that I
believe God wants us to have toward romance. What follows are five
important "new attitudes" that will help us break away from dating's
negative habits. Each of these flows from our view of three areas: love,
purity, and singleness. We'll expand on these three areas in the next
section, but for now the attitude changes described here give a
glimpse of the practical alternative God offers those who want to
please Him with their whole lives.

1. Every relationship is an opportunity to model Christ's love.

Bethany, an outgoing freshman at a Christian college, has a reputation
as a bit of a flirt. Unfortunately, much of her interaction with guys is
fake—it focuses on attracting attention to herself and getting a reaction from whoever she currently likes. Bethany invests more energy in
getting a guy to like her than she does in spurring him toward godliness.

But when Bethany changes her perspective and realizes her
friendships with guys are opportunities to love them as Christ does,
she takes a 180-degree turn from flirtatiousness to honest, sincere
love that treats guys as brothers, not potential boyfriends. Instead of
viewing herself as the center of the universe with other people revolving around her, she can begin to look for ways to bless others.

The world will know we follow Christ by the way we love others.
For this reason, we must practice love as God defines it—sincere,
servant-hearted, and selfless—not the world's brand of selfish and
sensual love based on what feels good.

2. My unmarried years are a gift from God.

Michael is twenty-one years old and has an engaging personality that
matches his good looks. As the intern for his church's youth ministry,

he has more than enough opportunities to meet and get to know Christian girls. Although he realizes his potential for ministry as a single and doesn't feel rushed to get married, he has developed a pattern of dating one girl after another. Although Michael has done nothing immoral, his pattern of short-term dating potentially robs him of the flexibility, freedom, and focus of singleness. He still operates from the old dating mindset that he's incomplete without a girlfriend.

But when Michael adopts a new attitude that views singleness as a gift, he learns to be content with friendship during the time God wants him to remain single. As a result, Michael can clear his life of the clutter that short-term relationships contribute. With this newly freed time and energy, Michael can pursue more effective ministry and deeper friendships with people of both genders.

Until you realize God's gift of your singleness, you'll probably miss out on the incredible opportunities it holds. Perhaps even now you can think of an opportunity you could grasp if you let go of the dating mindset. As a single you have the freedom right now to explore, study, and tackle the world. No other time in your life will offer these chances.

3. I DON'T NEED TO PURSUE A ROMANTIC RELATIONSHIP BEFORE I'M READY FOR MARRIAGE.

This new attitude grows out of the Little Relationship Principle we looked at in chapter 2: The joy of intimacy is the reward of commitment. Jenny is seventeen and has dated a boy from her church for over a year. They're both strong Christians, and they want to marry each other someday. The "someday" part is the problem—realistically, they can't get married for quite a few years. Both have specific things to accomplish for God before they can take that step.

The old attitude would say that intimacy feels good, so enjoy it now. But the new attitude recognizes that if two people can't make a commitment to each other, they don't have any business pursuing romance. Even though it isn't easy, Jenny tells her boyfriend that they need to limit the time and energy they invest in each other. Trusting that God can bring them back together if He wills, they halt their progression of intimacy until they can match it with commitment. Though they struggle with the separation, missing the closeness they once enjoyed, they know in the long run—whether they marry each other or someone else—they've made the best choice for both of them.

God has made each of us with a desire for intimacy, and He intends to fulfill it. While we're single He doesn't expect these long-ings to disappear, but I believe He asks us to have the patience to wait and, in the meantime, seek close relationships with family and deep, nonromantic relationships with brothers and sisters in the Lord.

This doesn't mean you have to marry the first person with whom you find both romance and intimacy. While I do know some people who have married the first person with whom they developed an inti-mate, romantic relationship, most of us won't follow this path. Each of us will probably develop close relationships with several people before God clearly indicates whom to marry. But we can't use this reality as an excuse to selfishly pursue romance for its own sake. I believe this mindset is misguided and selfish. If you're not ready to consider marriage or you're not truly interested in marrying a specific person, it's selfish and potentially very harmful to encourage that per-son to need you or ask him or her to gratify you emotionally or physically.

4. I CANNOT "OWN" SOMEONE OUTSIDE OF MARRIAGE.

In God's eyes two married people become one. And as you continue to mature, you'll often crave the oneness that comes from sharing life with someone. Perhaps you feel that desire even now. Yet I believe that until we're ready to commit our lives in marriage, we have no right to treat anyone as if he or she belongs to us.

Sarah and Philip are both seniors in high school and have gone out with each other for six months. Their relationship has reached a fairly serious level. In fact, for all intents and purposes, they might as well be married. They rarely do anything apart—they monopolize each other's weekends, drive each other's cars, and know each other's families almost as well as their own. Their physical relationship is also fairly serious. In fact, it's in a precarious position. Even though they haven't had sex, they constantly struggle with going too far.

The old attitude says we can "play marriage" if we really love someone. But the new attitude views a claim on another person's time, affection, and future before marriage as unwarranted.

Sarah and Philip realize they need to end their relationship as it now exists. By staking a claim on each other, they've stifled their individual growth and needlessly consumed energy that they should have directed into service and preparation for the future. They've planned their lives around each other when they don't really know that they'll get married someday. And in reality, if they're like most high school couples, there's a good chance they will probably marry someone else.

Even if Sarah and Philip had kept their physical relationship completely pure, they still would have made unwarranted claims on each other's spiritual and emotional lives by continuing the relationship. If God wants them together in the future, their current decision to halt their involvement won't endanger His plan. Right now they should choose to obey God and break up a relationship that has them stealing from each other.

Are you making unwarranted emotional, spiritual, or even physical claims on someone? Ask God to show you whether you need to reevaluate a current relationship.

5. I WILL AVOID SITUATIONS THAT COULD COMPROMISE THE PURITY OF MY BODY OR MIND.

Jessica, age sixteen, is a good girl who is unfortunately very naive. Even though she's a virgin and has committed to saving sex for marriage, she places herself in compromising situations with her older boyfriend—homework at her house when her mom's gone, hiking alone, ending their dates in his parked car. If Jessica were honest, she'd admit that she likes the excitement of these situations. She thinks it's very romantic, and it gives her a feeling of control over her boyfriend, who, to be quite honest, will go as far in their physical relationship as Jessica will allow.

But when Jessica takes on a new attitude, she sees that purity consists of more than remaining a virgin. When she honestly examines her relationship with her boyfriend, she realizes that she has veered from the *direction* of purity. To get back on course she has to drastically change her lifestyle. First she ends the relationship with her boyfriend because it focuses on the physical aspect. Then she commits to fleeing those settings that lend themselves to compromise.

Where, when, and with whom you choose to spend your time reveals your true commitment to purity. Do you need to examine your tendencies? If you do, make sure that you avoid placing yourself in settings that encourage temptation.

Unnecessary Baggage

Right now you might be thinking, *This new attitude is radical!* Maybe you're wondering whether you can adopt such seemingly foreign notions. I know that this new attitude challenges convention and even habits you may have already adopted. But I believe that if we want to live the "God-fashioned life," we must embrace a revolutionary pattern of living. The God-fashioned life leaves no room for pettiness, insincerity, wasted time, or selfishness. In short, it is a lifestyle that leaves no room for the seven habits of highly defective dating.

This may sound very difficult to you. To be honest, it is. Changing your attitude toward dating is something only God can help you do. But I can tell you from personal experience as well as from the example of many people I know that God can help you change—no matter how deeply ingrained your old attitudes might be.

And even though this might seem difficult, isn't there something in you that wants to live in this kind of radical obedience? The Christian with his or her eyes on the goal of sincere and intelligent love will find that throwing out the world's approach to relationships is no sacrifice. Rejecting the old attitude is the natural response not only to the evident problems in dating, but more important, to the high calling we've received from God. He commands us to "throw off everything that hinders" and "run with perseverance the race marked out for us" (Hebrews 12:1). But what's the alternative? you ask. Loneliness? Lifelong singleness? Friday nights at home watching videos with your cat? No! No! No!

Choosing to quit the dating game doesn't mean rejecting friendship with the opposite sex, companionship, romance, or marriage. We still can pursue these things; we just choose to pursue them on God's terms and in His time. God asks us to put our romantic ambitions in the "all these things" pile that we must leave behind so we can "seek first his kingdom and his righteousness" (Matthew 6:33). Leaving dating behind is a by-product of God's primary desire for us to consume ourselves with seeking Him wholeheartedly.

Making the Trade

So let me ask you some soul-searching questions. Are you willing to break our culture's rules to experience God's best? Are you willing to give Him everything, committing yourself to Him with abandon?

A simple story told by one of my favorite preachers, Ravi Zacharias, clearly illustrates the choice we face. One day a boy who has a bag of marbles proposes a trade with a little girl who has a bag of candy. The girl gladly agrees. But as the boy gets out his marbles, he realizes that he can't bear to part with some of them. Rather dishonestly, he takes three of his best marbles and hides them under his pillow. The boy and girl make the trade, and the girl never knows he has cheated her. But that night while the girl lies fast asleep, the boy has no peace. He's wide awake, pondering a question that nags at him: "I wonder if she kept her best candy, too?"

Like that little boy, many of us walk through life plagued by the question "Has God given me His best?" But the question that we must answer first is "Am I giving God *my* best?"

You and I will never experience God's best—in singleness or in marriage—until we give God our all. We've held on to old attitudes, foolishly clutching a lifestyle that the world tells us will bring fulfillment. God asks us to hand it all over to Him.

Where are you right now? Have you given God everything within you, or do you still hold your favorite marbles in your hands, including your attitude about dating?

In the following chapters we'll examine our attitudes toward three heart issues—love, purity, and singleness—that shape our approach to relationships. As we seek to gain God's perspective, we'll discover that giving Him everything is well worth the trade.

PART TWO

The Heart of

the Matter

CHAPTER FIVE

Looking Up "Love" in God's Dictionary

Learning the True Definition of Love

YOU DID WHAT?" I asked in disbelief.

Jeff laughed loudly and accelerated the car as we went around a turn. My shock apparently energized him. "Gloria told her mom she was staying at her friend's house, and we rented a room at a hotel last Friday night," he said, as if it were no big deal.

Jeff and his girlfriend, Gloria, had been going out for a while. If you didn't count the numerous times they had broken up then reconciled, they had dated for almost a year. Jeff had always remained vague about their level of physical involvement, but now they had obviously fully consummated their relationship.

"We got a room at the Holiday Inn," he explained as he put his hand out the window into the cool night air. Turning to me he grinned, winked mischievously, and said, "Man, oh, man."

"I can't believe you," I said, letting the tone of my voice convey my disapproval. "You mean you and Gloria had…you had…I mean, you slept together?"

Jeff could tell I wasn't pleased. He wanted me to be impressed, to slap him on the back like one of his football teammates in the locker room and praise him for his "exploit." I wanted to slap him all right, but not on the back.

"Look, Josh," he said defensively, "we waited a long time for this. It was really special. Maybe it doesn't meet your morals, but we felt that it was the right time to show our love."

"My morals?" I said indignantly. "My morals? Since when are they mine? How many times have we talked about this? With each other? At church? Jeff, you know that wasn't right. You…"

"We love each other," Jeff said, cutting me off midsentence. "If you ever really fall in love, then you'll understand."

The conversation ended. For some reason the stoplight took forever to turn green. We sat silently as the turn signal clicked off and on. I looked out the window.

Four years later, Jeff was going to college in Michigan. "I'm engaged!" he told me over the phone. "Debbie is incredible. I've never been so in love."

"That's great," I said. My congratulations sounded hollow. I couldn't help it. I was thinking of Gloria. I hadn't seen her for a long time. Where was she now? Three or four girlfriends back? Love, huh?

The First Kiss

"How does Chinese sound?" I asked as we pulled out of the driveway.

"Hey, that's great," Eric replied with his typical enthusiasm.

I'd only just met Eric and his wife, Leslie, but had already noted Eric's exuberance and excitement about everything—even my restaurant suggestion.

"That all right with you, honey?" he gently asked Leslie, who was sitting in the backseat.

"Sure," she replied sweetly.

Eric and Leslie had stopped by to visit me during a drive through the Northwest. A friend in Colorado had told me about these newlyweds and the little book they had written called *His Perfect Faithfulness*. Their book told the story of how they had met and grown to love each other without following the typical pattern of dating.

You'd be hard pressed to find two more romantic people. They adored each other, and it showed. Eric rarely took his eyes off Leslie. Sitting in the passenger seat on the way to the restaurant, he slipped his hand behind the seat, and Leslie reached forward and clasped it. Holding hands when one person is sitting in the front seat and the other is in the back? I'd never seen that before.

After dinner, while we cracked open our fortune cookies, I had a question. "You two can't keep your hands off each other," I began teasingly. Leslie blushed. "Was it difficult keeping the physical side of your relationship pure while you were engaged?"

Eric took Leslie's hand and smiled at her before he answered. "Of course the desire for that was present—it always will be," he said. "But no, it wasn't a struggle. Leslie and I decided very early in our relationship that we were going to refrain from physical contact until we were married. Our first kiss was at the altar."

My jaw dropped. "You didn't kiss until you got married?"

"Nope," Eric said, beaming. "The most we did was hold hands. And Josh, we know that kind of standard isn't for every couple. We didn't make that decision to be legalistic; it came from the heart. Everyone, even our parents, told us we should kiss. But we both decided waiting was what we wanted to do. It was a way to show our love, to protect each other before we were married." And then with a twinkle in his eye he said, "Let me tell you, Josh, that first kiss was the most incredible, beautiful thing in the world. I can't even begin to describe it."

Eric and Leslie. Jeff and Gloria. Two couples that used the same word—*love*—to explain what motivated them to act in opposite ways. Were both couples talking about the same thing? For Jeff and Gloria, love justified a night in a hotel room enjoying each other's bodies before marriage. For Eric and Leslie, love meant barely touching each other before they met at the altar. For Jeff and Gloria, love was impatient and demanded compromise. For Eric and Leslie, love fueled integrity and gave them the patience needed to wait.

One word. Two definitions.

In Love with Love

I am, by my own admission, a hopeless romantic. If such a thing is possible, I am in love with being in love.

There's nothing else quite like it, and if you've experienced it, you know what I mean. Being in love is a patchwork of a thousand indescribable moments. Nervous energy runs through your body whenever you think of that special person, which is every waking minute. You lose interest in the dull chores of eating, sleeping, and thinking rationally. You discover that every love song on the radio was written for you. It seems that someone has removed blinders from your eyes and you can see the world full of wonder and mystery and happiness.

I love love. But I've come to realize that I don't really know much about it. Oh, I can tell you all about the warm, fuzzy side of love. I can throw myself into romance with all the passion of Romeo, but in God's school of true love, I'm afraid I'm still in kindergarten.

To me and other romantics who share a "love for love," God wants to give us a higher, grander view. He wants to deepen our understanding. Romance can thrill us to our core, but it's only a small part of true love. We've been playing in the sandbox; God wants to take us to the beach.

Aphrodite or Christ?

I cannot overemphasize the importance of gaining God's perspective on love. We can link all the problems in relationships today to adopting a fallen world's attitudes toward love. And the conflict between God's definition of love and the world's is not new. Christians have always had a choice to either imitate the Master or slip into the more enticing pattern of love provided by the world.

The apostle Paul understood this struggle when he wrote his famous chapter on love to the Christians living in Corinth (see 1 Corinthians 13). He must have realized the irony of his task. In Paul's day, writing to Corinthians about God's love was the equivalent of writing a letter on family values to Hollywood today. *Corinthian* was synonymous with immorality. To "play the Corinthian" meant to give oneself to sexual pleasure. A "Corinthian girl" was another word for a prostitute. How could Paul hope to convey an understanding of God's pure love to a city steeped in perversion?

> Love is patient, love is kind. It does not envy, it does not boast, it is not proud. (1 Corinthians 13:4)

The bustling, cosmopolitan port town had elevated sex to a religious pursuit. The temple of Aphrodite, the Greek goddess of love, employed one thousand prostitutes. How could these people possibly understand the true meaning of the statement "God is love" (1 John 4:16) when on every street corner and from every brothel someone offered their version of "love"—sensual pleasure—to them? Would they see the truth and beauty of real love in the midst of the seductiveness of its counterfeit?

> It is not rude, it is not self-seeking, it is not easily angered, it keeps no record of wrongs. (1 Corinthians 13:5)

Would Aphrodite or Christ triumph in Corinth? Would sensuality push out servanthood? Would sexuality have priority over selflessness? Would the readers of Paul's humble letter choose the everlasting, or the fleeting pleasure of the moment?

Christians today endure the very same struggle. Though separated by some two thousand years, our culture and that of Corinth share many similarities. More than ever, sex is a commodity. Sensuality and exaggerated sexuality shout at us on every corner—if not from brothels, then from newsstands, billboards, and websites. "Love is sex," a magazine ad whispers. "Sex is pleasure," a movie tells us. And on the radio, "Pleasure is all that matters" is sung sweetly in our ears.

In the midst of this harangue from the world, God's quiet

message of true love still speaks to those who choose to listen.

Can you hear it? Put down the magazine. Turn off the television. Pull the plug on the stereo and listen…

Love does not delight in evil but rejoices with the truth. It always protects, always trusts, always hopes, always perseveres. Love never fails. (1 Corinthians 13:6–8)

Fashion Nightmare

Like the Christians in Corinth, we have two styles of love to select from—God's or the world's. Which will we choose?

Here's an image that may help us understand our role as followers of Christ and the style of love we should therefore adopt. You may think it sounds strange at first, but stick with me. It will make sense as I explain. I think we should view love as something we wear.

From the day Adam and Eve disobeyed God then donned fig leaves in the Garden of Eden, the world has experienced something of a fashion nightmare, not in terms of clothing but in terms of love. When sin marred God's original design for love, the human race began "wearing" a twisted, corrupted imitation based on selfishness and irresponsibility.

But because God's love is perfect and enduring, He created a way for us to experience His design for love once again. He sent His Son, Jesus Christ, to set things straight. In fashion terms, we could call the Author and Finisher of our faith the Designer and Model of a revolutionary expression of love. Christ gave His life for a world that rejected Him, and He told us to love our enemies. He washed the feet of the men who called him Master and told us to serve each other in humility.

He gave us the pattern— "As I have loved you, so you must love one another" (John 13:34)—and told us to share it with the world.

Supermodels

We may never model high fashion in New York or Paris, but as Christians we model God's love to the world. Understanding this role profoundly affects our approach to relationships, especially our dating relationships. When dating, we represent God's love, not only to the other person in the relationship, but also to the people watching us.

As Christians, we need to remember that God's perfect love is not only for our benefit. A model wears clothing to attract attention to the designer's creativity. The model displays the designer's work, but the designer's reputation, not the model's, is on the line. In the same way, as Christians, we model God's love, whether or not we realize it. People watch us, and what they see affects God's reputation for loving His creation. If we claim to follow Christ then wear the world's twisted style of love, we drag the name and character of our Lord in the dirt.

For this reason, we must ask ourselves, "Am I modeling the love of Christ? Do my motivations and actions in this relationship reflect the perfect love God has shown me?" How would you answer those questions right now?

I Love Me

I believe that we can better model God's perfect love when we avoid the negative habits of dating. And doing this requires recognizing and rejecting the world's pattern of love. First we must understand that all of the world's deceptions flow from the belief that *love is primarily for the fulfillment and comfort of self.* The world poisons love by focusing first and foremost on meeting one's own needs.

We witness this poison in the boyfriend or girlfriend who pressures a partner into sex. You've heard the line "If you really loved me, you'd do it." In other words, "I don't care about you, your convictions, or how this could hurt you—satisfy *my* desire!" Or what about the person who dates someone because it will boost his or her popularity but then dumps that person when someone in a higher social stratum comes along? While the first example is more extreme, both examples illustrate self-centered "love" in action.

Next we're told that *love is primarily a feeling*. At first glance this seems innocent enough—we often *feel* love, and this isn't necessarily wrong. But when we make our feelings the most important measure of love, we place *ourselves* at the center of importance. Our feelings by themselves don't do others one bit of good. If a man feels love for the poor but never gives money to help them or never shows kindness to them, what are his feelings worth? They may benefit him, but if his actions don't communicate love, his feelings mean nothing.

By inflating the importance of feelings, we neglect the importance of putting love in action. When we evaluate the quality of our love for someone else simply by our own emotional fulfillment, we are being selfish.

Out of Control

The third common fallacy about love deals with personal responsibility. The world tells us that *love is beyond our control*.

This thinking has found its way into our language. We describe the beginning of a passionate relationship as "falling in love." Or people say, "We're madly in love with each other." You've more than likely heard people say these things—perhaps you've even said them yourself.

Why do we feel compelled to compare love to a pit or a mental disorder? What do these statements reveal about our attitudes toward love? I think part of the reason we make these somewhat overstated analogies is because they remove personal responsibility. If a person falls into a pit, what can she do about it? If an animal contracts rabies and runs around foaming at the mouth and biting people, it can't really help its nasty behavior because it has gone mad.

Doesn't it sound a little absurd to discuss love in such terms? I think so. Yet we tend to express our experience of love in these ways. We think of love as something beyond our control and thus excuse ourselves from having to behave responsibly. In extreme cases, people have blamed love for immorality, murder, rape, and many other sins. Okay, so maybe you and I haven't done those things. But perhaps you've lied to parents or friends because of a relationship. Maybe you pushed your partner too far physically. But if love is out of our control, we can't possibly be held responsible. Yes, we know we behaved rashly. Yes, we know we might have hurt others in the process, but we couldn't help it. We were in love.

A Slap in the Face

The world may define and defend love in these terms, but the Bible offers a very different perspective. For the person practicing the self-centered, feelings-governed, beyond-my-control love of the world, God's definition can be as startling as an unexpected slap in the face.

The world takes us to a silver screen on which flickering images of passion and romance play, and as we watch, the world says, "This is love." God takes us to the foot of a tree on which a naked and bloodied man hangs and says, "*This* is love."

God always defines love by pointing to His Son. This was the only way our sins could be forgiven. The innocent One took the place of the guilty—He offered himself up to death so that we could have eternal life. God's perfect love for a fallen world is most clearly seen in the death of His Son.

And all who find forgiveness and life through Jesus are called to follow in His steps—to love others because He first loved us (1 John 4:19). Christ's antidote to the poison of self-love is the Cross. "If anyone would come after me," Jesus said, "he must deny himself and take up his cross and follow me" (Matthew 16:24).

Christ taught that *love is not for the fulfillment of self but for the glory of God and the good of others*. True love is selfless. It gives; it sacrifices; it dies to its own needs. "Greater love has no one than this," Jesus said, "that he lay down his life for his friends" (John 15:13). He backed up His words with actions—He laid down His life for all of us.

Christ also showed that *true love is not measured or governed by feeling.* He went to the cross when every emotion and instinct in His body told Him to turn back. Have you ever read about the night before Jesus' death when He prayed in the Garden of Gethsemane? (See Mark 14:32.) He clearly didn't *feel* like enduring the beatings, hanging on the cross, and enduring God's wrath for sin. But He submitted Himself to His Father's will. Jesus' feelings were not the test of His love, nor were they His master.

Christ wants us to have this same attitude. He did not say, "If you love me, you will feel warm, cascading sensations of religious emotion." Instead He told us, "If you love me, you will obey what I command" (John 14:15). True love always expresses itself in obedience to God and service to others. Good feelings are nice but not necessary.

Jesus' example also shows us that *love is under our control.* He *chose* to love us. He chose to lay down His life for us. The danger of believing that you "fall in love" is that it also means you can "fall out of love" just as unexpectedly. Aren't you glad that God's love for us isn't as unpredictable? Aren't you thankful that God's love is under His control and not based on whim? We need to throw out the misconception that love is some strange "force" that tosses us around against our will like leaves in the wind. We cannot justify doing what we know is wrong by saying that love grabbed hold of us and "made" us behave irresponsibly. That's not love. Instead, it's what the Bible calls in 1 Thessalonians 4:5 "passionate lust." We express true love in obedience to God and service to others—not reckless or selfish behavior—and we *choose* these behaviors.

Practical Change

With these truths about love in place, let's make a practical application. If dating hinges on our attitude toward love, what happens to dating when we take on Christ's attitudes?

Sparks fly.

God's true love clashes with dating as we know it. Think about it—when you date guided by the world's attitude that love is for the benefit of self, you base your dating decisions on what's best for you. I opened this chapter with a story about my friends Jeff and Gloria. Unfortunately, they often subscribed to the world's definition of love. First, their motivation was self-centered. Jeff went out with Gloria because she was pretty, other guys liked her, and she satisfied him sexually. His criteria for pursuing a relationship with her could be compared to his criteria for choosing a pair of jeans—makes me feel good, makes me look good. But Gloria wasn't much better. She liked Jeff because he was a "prize"—he was good-looking and athletic, and he owned a nice car. They satisfied each other's sinful desires and helped each other's image.

But had they turned away from the world's self-centered attitude, many of the "good reasons" for pursuing romance in dating would have begun to disappear. What if Jeff and Gloria had asked, "What is my *real* reason for seeing this person romantically? What am I seeking that couldn't be found in a friendship? Am I selfishly seeking only my own fulfillment? What am I communicating to him (or her)? Am I arousing emotions I'm not ready to meet with equal commitment? Is this relationship going to help or hinder his (or her) walk with God? Will he (or she) be hurt if I allow this relationship to proceed right now?"

We need to start asking ourselves these kinds of questions. Is this other-focused attitude more complicated? Maybe. More godly? Definitely. When we extract the poison of self-love, our entire motivation in relationships is transformed.

More changes occur when we seek to love with Christ's love. Jeff and Gloria bought into the world's assumption that love was beyond their control. Their feelings governed their actions. They were enslaved to what 1 John 2:16 calls the "cravings of sinful man" and "the lust of his eyes." They often used "being in love" as an excuse for disobeying God. In their physical relationship, they grabbed at all they could within (and ultimately outside) the boundaries set for couples before marriage. They ended up lying to their parents and violating each other's purity, all in the name of love. Feelings governed them, and finally, when the feelings ended so did their relationship.

But what if Jeff and Gloria had realized that they would answer to God for their actions—regardless of whether or not they were "in love"? They probably would have told their feelings to take a hike.

The same is true for you and me. We need to forget our sinful instincts! By nature, our instincts want to set us on a course for destruction. Our feelings can lie to us. We shouldn't allow them to set the tone or the pace for our relationships. Instead, we need to allow God's Word and patience and selflessness to guide us.

"Love Must Be Sincere"

As we seek to love according to God's design, we must pursue sincerity: "Love must be sincere." This brief command given in Romans 12:9 leaves no room for misunderstanding. The love God wants His children to live by has no room for deceit and hypocrisy—it has to be genuine and earnest.

Unfortunately, much of what takes place between guys and girls today is insincere. There is nearly always an angle, a hidden agenda: *What can you do for me? What can I get from you?*

I'll never forget a conversation I sat through with a group of guys. Girls, you would have been appalled if you had overheard it. These guys were discussing things a guy could do on a date to get a girl to fall for him. They recited lines for stirring the heart and lines for getting a kiss. One guy explained his technique of alternating warmth with disinterest and coolness—he claimed that this approach kept a girl guessing and trying her best to please him. Another guy shared ways to put a girl in a romantic mood. He'd take a date to a furniture store, and as he and the girl walked through the displays, he would talk about families and ask which tables and couches she would want for her home someday. "Girls go nuts for this!" he told us. He explained that with marriage and future plans on her mind, the girl would more likely be romantic and affectionate during the evening.

This conversation was a study in manipulation. All of it was completely fake, completely insincere. These guys weren't seeking ways to bless girls. They merely wanted to push emotional buttons to get something for themselves.

I'm sure many girls would admit to having their own set of tricks. But no matter how commonplace or ingrained in our culture these practices may be, we all face judgment by the four simple words given by God: "Love must be sincere."

We need to embrace the incredible responsibility we bear as representatives of Christ's love here on earth. "By this all men will know that you are my disciples," Jesus said, "if you love one another" (John 13:35). The world will know we are different and get a glimpse of God's divine, saving love by the way we love. Will others see the sincerity of Christ's love in our relationships? Or will they see the same brand of self-centered love practiced by the world and turn away in disappointment?

Practice Makes Perfect— or Perfectly Imperfect

The love we practice in dating not only shows the world Christ's love; it also prepares us for our future relationships. As we relate to others today, we form patterns that we'll take with us into our marriages. For this reason, we must practice not only sincere love but also commitment-based love.

We see so much divorce and betrayal in our society today. Take a quick count—how many of your friends come from broken homes? I believe that this trend will only increase as each generation begins to practice short-term love in dating relationships earlier and earlier. It seems that dating as we have come to know it doesn't really prepare us for marriage; instead it can be a training ground for divorce. We cannot practice lifelong commitment in a series of short-term relationships.

Does that mean we're supposed to marry the first person we date? No. We need to carefully and cautiously consider marriage, remaining willing to back out of a relationship if God shows us we need to. There's no wisdom in rushing into marriage simply because we've become romantically attached to someone.

The wrong mindset that is so prevalent today, however, is not related to choosing a spouse. Many of us have fallen prey to the idea that we can and should pursue romance for its own sake. In other words, "I'll become intimate with you because it feels good, not because I'm prayerfully considering marriage." This attitude is not fair to the other person and is terrible preparation for marriage. Who wants to marry someone who will ditch a relationship the moment romantic feelings wane? Who wants to marry a person who has developed a habit of breaking up and finding someone new when the going gets tough?

We need to realize that the lifelong commitment so many of us desire in our future marriages cannot be practiced or prepared for in a lifestyle of short-term relationships. Until we can commit to making a relationship work for the rest of our lives—and yes, it is a huge commitment—we do ourselves and others a disservice by pursuing short-term love in the meantime. True love waits, but not just for sex. It waits for the right time to commit to God's brand of love—unwavering, unflagging, and totally committed.

Pushing Out Pettiness

Committed, sincere, selfless, responsible—all these words describe God's love. And each stands in stark contrast to the love practiced by the world.

Maybe some ideas in this chapter have sparked your interest and you're wondering, "How should I respond?" Here are some ideas. You may find them challenging; perhaps you'll disagree with them. But I must clearly state my convictions here. In my view, if our habits in dating encourage us to wear the world's style of love, then dating as we know it needs to go. If dating causes us to practice selfish, feelings-governed love that's contrary to God's love, we must be willing to reject it. God's grand view of love pushes out the pettiness and selfish-

ness that defines so much of what takes place in relationships today.
We cannot love as God loves and date as the world dates. It's time to
let His definition of love redefine the way we live.

CHAPTER SIX

The Right Thing at the Wrong Time Is the Wrong Thing

How to Keep Impatience from Robbing You of the Gift of Singleness

IN *THE BOOK OF VIRTUES*, William J. Bennett tells a story called "The Magic Thread." In this French tale we read of Peter, a boy who is strong and able, yet sadly flawed by an attitude of impatience. Always dissatisfied with his present condition, Peter spends his life daydreaming about the future.

One day while wandering in the forest, Peter meets a strange old woman who gives him a most tantalizing opportunity—the chance to skip the dull, mundane moments of life. She hands Peter a silver ball from which a tiny gold thread protrudes. "This is your life thread," she explains. "Do not touch it and time will pass normally. But if you wish time to pass more quickly, you have only to pull the thread a little way and an hour will pass like a second. But I warn you, once the thread has been pulled out, it cannot be pushed back in again."

This magical thread seems the answer to all of Peter's problems. It is just what he has always wanted. He takes the ball and runs home.

The following day in school Peter has his first opportunity to put the silver ball to use. The lesson is dragging, and the teacher scolds Peter for not concentrating. Peter fingers the silver ball and gives the thread a slight tug. Suddenly the teacher dismisses the class, and Peter is free to leave school. He is overjoyed! How easy his life will now be. From this moment, Peter begins to pull the thread a little every day.

But soon Peter begins to use the magic thread to rush through larger portions of life. Why waste time pulling the thread just a little every day when he can pull it hard and complete school altogether? He does so and finds himself out of school and apprenticed in a trade. Peter uses the same technique to rush through his engagement to his sweetheart. He cannot bear to wait months to marry her, so he uses the gold thread to hasten the arrival of his wedding day.

Peter continues this pattern throughout his life. When hard, trying times come, he escapes them with his magic thread. When the baby cries at night, when he faces financial struggles, when he wishes his own children to be launched in careers of their own, Peter pulls the magic thread and bypasses the discomfort of the moment.

But sadly, when he comes to the end of his life, Peter realizes the emptiness of such an existence. By allowing impatience and discontentment to rule him, Peter has robbed himself of life's richest moments and memories. With only the grave to look forward to, he deeply regrets ever having used the magic thread.

In introducing this story, Mr. Bennett insightfully comments, "Too often, people want what they want (or what they *think* they want, which is usually "happiness" in one form or another) *right now*. The irony of their impatience is that only by learning to wait, and by a willingness to accept the bad with the good, do we usually attain those things that are truly worthwhile."

Does Impatience Dictate Our Dating?

I think we can gain valuable insight from Mr. Bennett's words as we examine the attitudes that often guide dating. As we apply his words to the subject of this book, we move from the ethereal topic of love to the more concrete subject of timing. *When* we pursue romance is a major factor in determining whether or not dating is appropriate for us. And we can only determine the appropriate time to pursue romance when we understand God's purpose for singleness and trust *His* timing for relationships.

Though it isn't true of all relationships, dating relationships are often fueled by impatience, and we can directly relate many problems with dating to wrong timing. We want what we want right now. While we don't possess a magical gold thread to rush us through life, we can develop wrong attitudes that have a similar effect. But God wants us to appreciate the gifts of the present season of our lives. He wants us to learn the patience and trust necessary to wait for His perfect timing in all things, including our love lives. Let's examine three simple truths that can help correct wrong attitudes about the timing of relationships.

I. THE RIGHT THING AT THE WRONG TIME IS THE WRONG THING.

In today's world we don't readily accept the concept of delayed gratification. Our culture teaches us that if something is good, we should seek to enjoy it immediately. So we microwave our food, e-mail our letters, and express mail our packages. We do our best to escape the confines of time by accelerating our schedules, speeding up our pace, and doing whatever it takes to beat the clock. You probably know exactly what I mean. How did you respond the last time you had to wait in line for something? Did you patiently wait your turn, or did you tap your toe and try to rush the experience?

Our "do it all now" mentality has tremendously affected the timing of today's dating relationships. We see this in headlines about kids having sex at an increasingly young age. As young people rush prematurely into these activities that God has reserved for marriage, most of their elders do little to correct them. After all, what can adults say when they live by the same attitude?

Why do we insist on living this way? In my opinion, part of the reason we've adopted the immediate gratification mentality is because we've lost sight of the biblical principle of seasons (see Ecclesiastes 3:1–8). Just as spring's role is different from that of fall, so each of the seasons of our lives has a different emphasis, focus, and beauty. One is not better than another; each season yields its own unique treasures. We cannot skip ahead to experience the riches of another life season any more than a farmer can rush the spring. Each season builds on the one before it.

God has many wonderful experiences He wants to give to us, but He also assigns these experiences to particular seasons of our lives. We often make the mistake, however, of taking a good thing out of its appropriate season to enjoy it when *we* want it. Premarital sex is a prime example of this. Sex in itself is a wonderful experience (from what my married friends tell me), but if we indulge in it outside of God's plan, we sin (1 Corinthians 6:18–20). Like a fruit picked green or a flower plucked before it blossoms, our attempts to rush God's timing can spoil the beauty of His plan for our lives.

Just because something is good doesn't mean we should pursue it right now. We have to remember that the right thing at the wrong time is the wrong thing.

2. YOU DON'T NEED TO SHOP FOR WHAT YOU CAN'T AFFORD.

The timing of many dating relationships is equivalent to going shopping for an outfit when you don't have any money; even if you find the "perfect fit," what can you do about it?

This is an example of how the Little Relationship Principle we talked about in chapter 2 can help us with issues of timing. Do you remember the principle? *The joy of intimacy is the reward of commitment.* How does this help us determine whether our dating is premature shopping for something we can't afford? Think of restating the principle this way: "Intimacy costs commitment. If I'm not in a position to pay in the cold, hard cash of commitment, I have no business going shopping for my future mate."

Before two people are ready for the responsibility of commitment, they should content themselves with friendship and wait on deep emotional intimacy. Exercising this patience will not handicap them relationally. In friendship, they can practice the skills of relating, caring, and sharing their lives with other people. In friendship, they can observe other people's characters and begin to see what they'll one day want in their mates. While it's true we can learn worthwhile lessons from dating relationships, we need to make sure those relationships don't bog us down. Wasting too much time trying each other out as boyfriend and girlfriend can actually distract two people from the more important task of preparing to be good spouses.

God has a perfect plan for your life. More than likely, that plan includes marriage, and if so, somewhere in this world God has the perfect person for you. You may or may not know this person right now. If you spend all your time and energy trying to hunt this person down or (if you've already found this person) trying to contain him or her until you can marry, you might actually do that person a disservice. We'll talk later in the book about how we can be making the most of the season of waiting. For now what's most important to realize is that the guy or girl you will one day marry doesn't need a girlfriend or boyfriend (even though he or she may want one right now). What that person really needs is someone mature enough to spend the season before marriage preparing to be a godly wife or husband.

Let's do our future spouses a favor and stop shopping around prematurely.

3. ANY SEASON OF SINGLENESS IS A GIFT FROM GOD.

Most of us won't remain single for our entire lives, and I think that we should view our singleness as a special season of our lives, a gift from God. God gives an outline for the proper attitude toward singleness in 1 Corinthians 7:32. *The Message* translation reads:

> I want you to live as free of complications as possible. When you're unmarried, you're free to concentrate on simply pleasing the Master. Marriage involves you in all the nuts and

bolts of domestic life and in wanting to please your spouse, leading to so many more demands on your attention. The time and energy that married people spend on caring for and nurturing each other, the unmarried can spend in becoming…holy instruments of God.

Paul doesn't say this to put marriage down. He says it to encourage us to view singleness as a gift. God doesn't use our singleness to punish us. He has created this season as an unparalleled opportunity for undistracted devotion to God. And as a time for growth and service that we shouldn't take for granted or allow to slip by.

One person rightly stated, "Don't do something about your singlehood—do something *with* it!" Stop for just a minute and evaluate whether you're using God's gift of singleness as He desires. Ask yourself these questions:

- Am I concentrating on "simply pleasing the Master"?
- Am I using this season of my life to become a "holy" instrument for God?
- Or am I scrambling to find a romantic relationship with someone by dating?
- Am I failing to believe that God is sovereign over this part of my life and can provide for me?
- Could I possibly be throwing away the gift of singleness?
- Am I cluttering my life with needless complications and worries of dating?

While we're single, dating not only keeps us from preparing for marriage, but can also quite possibly rob us of the gift of singleness. Dating can tie us down in a series of pseudo relationships, but God wants us to maximize our freedom and flexibility to serve Him. Any season of singleness, whether you're sixteen or fifty-six, is a gift. You just might do God a disservice by wasting its potential on a lifestyle of short-term dating.

Do You Really Trust Him?

Though simply stated, these three truths can bring about radical lifestyle changes when we apply them to our lives. To do so requires us to wait. That's right—God just asks us to wait. You might not find that idea bold or daring or very impressive, but it is obedient, and our obedience catches God's attention (2 Chronicles 16:9).

Waiting for God's timing requires trusting in His goodness and wisdom. We develop patience as we trust that God denies us what we think is good only because He has something better for us—both now and in the future.

I'll freely admit it—I often have difficulty trusting God. When it comes to my love life, I have a nagging fear that He wants to keep me single forever. Or I fear that if He lets me marry, He'll match me up with some girl to whom I won't feel attracted.

I know these worries are silly. In my better moments I admit I haven't based these fears on the reality of the loving, caring Father in heaven that I've come to know. But even though I know He's a good God, I often allow my lack of faith to affect the way I approach dating.

I fear that God might forget me. Instead of trusting in His perfect timing, I often try to take things into my own hands. I grab my life's calendar from God and frantically begin to pencil in my own plans and agendas. "God, I know You're omnipotent and all that," I say, "but I really think You missed the fact that this girl over here is my destiny. If I don't go after her now, my future will pass me by!" Eventually I sheepishly hand back the scheduling of my time, energy, and attention, saying, "Of course I trust You, Lord, but I just think You could use a little help."

Dating and Marshmallows

An article in *Time* magazine left this indelible image in my mind: a little child sitting alone in a room, staring at a marshmallow. This strange picture captures the feelings I sometimes have in my struggle to trust God to take care of my future marital status.

The article's subject was unrelated to dating—and marshmallows, too, for that matter. It was about research done with children. The first few paragraphs went this way:

It turns out that a scientist can see the future by watching four-year-olds interact with a marshmallow. The researcher invites the children, one by one, into a plain room and begins the gentle torment. "You can have this marshmallow right now," he says. "But if you wait while I run an errand, you can have two marshmallows when I get back." And then he leaves.

Some children grab the treat the minute he's out the door. Some last a few minutes before they give in. But others are determined to wait. They cover their eyes; they put their heads down; they sing to themselves; they try to play games or even fall asleep. When the researcher returns, he gives these children their hard-earned marshmallows. And then, science waits for them to grow up.

By the time the children reach high school, something remarkable has happened. A survey of the children's parents and teachers found that those who as four-year-olds had the fortitude to hold out for the second marshmallow generally grew up to be better adjusted, more popular, adventurous, confident and dependable teenagers. The children who gave in to temptation early on were more likely to be lonely, easily frustrated and stubborn. They buckled under stress and shied away from challenges.

Of course, the moral of the story is that developing the character necessary to delay gratification in small areas can translate into great success in other areas. But the four-year-olds in the study didn't know that. They didn't resist the marshmallow in hopes of getting better grades in high school. They overcame their urge to eat the marshmallow because they had faith—they could envision the moment when the nice man in the white coat would come back with *two* marshmallows. They persevered because they trusted.

This story really encourages me. Sometimes as I wait on God's timing for romance, I go through the same internal struggle those kids must have endured. Like a marshmallow beckoning the child to eat its sweet fluffiness, dating is calling my name. And let me tell you, it looks *good.*

Why don't I snatch it up? Why shouldn't you? Because God has promised something better. He provides something better *now* as we take advantage of the unique opportunities of singleness, and He'll provide something better *later* when we enter into marriage. But we must have faith to believe it. Like those little children, we're left alone with something that we *think* could satisfy us immediately. And we can't see the reward of delaying our gratification.

It gets down to this question: Do you trust God? Don't just give a knee-jerk, Sunday school answer. Do you *really* trust Him? Do you live your life as if you trust Him? Do you believe that by passing up something good now because it's the *wrong time,* God will bring you something better when it is the *right time?*

Jim and Elisabeth Elliot faced this difficult question in their passionate relationship. They loved each other deeply, yet they placed God's will before their own desires. In *Passion and Purity,* Mrs. Elliot writes:

> We were being asked to leave the planning to God. God's ultimate plan was as far beyond our imaginings as the oak tree is from the acorn's imaginings. The acorn does what it was made to do, without pestering its Maker with questions about when and how and why. We who have been given an intelligence and a will and a whole range of wants that can be set against the divine Pattern for Good are asked to believe Him. We are given the chance to trust Him when He says to us, "…If any man will let himself be lost for my sake, he will find his true self."

When will we find it? we ask. The answer is, *Trust Me.*

How will we find it? The answer again is, *Trust Me.*

Why must I let myself be lost? we persist. The answer is, *Look at the acorn and trust Me.*

God Knew Best

Many people realize too late that we don't arrive at contentment as a destination as much as we develop contentment as a state of mind. Paul tells us in 1 Timothy 6:6 that "godliness with contentment is great gain." And in Philippians 4:11 he writes, "I have learned to be content whatever the circumstances." What is Paul's secret?

Paul shares it with us: "I can do everything through him who gives me strength" (Philippians 4:13). Paul trusted God to give him strength to endure *any* situation he faced. In the same way, we can gain contentment when we trust in God's strength and grace to sustain us through any circumstance. Whether you're single or married, whether you're liked, loved, or lonely, the key to contentment is trust. Believe it or not, if we are discontented with singleness, we'll more than likely face discontentment when we're married. When we define our happiness by some point in the future, it will never arrive. We'll keep waiting until tomorrow. If we allow impatience to govern us, we will miss the gift of the moment. We'll arrive at that point in time we expected to provide fulfillment and find it lacking.

One lady wrote to me, frustrated that people often view a single woman as just marking time until the right man comes along. "Poor single woman!" she continued. "The world wants her to fornicate, and the church wants her to marry! Whatever happened to what Paul said about the blessings of being single? William Booth, the founder of the Salvation Army, wrote, 'Don't instill, or allow anybody else to instill into the hearts of your girls the idea that marriage is the chief end of life. If you do, don't be surprised if they get engaged to the first empty, useless fool they come across.' Women (and men) should marry when it is plainly the will of God for their lives, not because they 'can't minister' otherwise, or because of social pressure." I can only add a hearty "Amen!" to her comments.

Author John Fischer, speaking as a single, young adult said:

> God has called me to live now, not four years from now. He wants me to realize my full potential as a man right now, to be thankful for that, and to enjoy it to the fullest. I have a feeling that a single person who is always wishing he were married will probably get married, discover all that is involved, and wish he were single again. He will ask himself, "Why didn't I use that time, when I didn't have so many other obligations, to serve the Lord? Why didn't I give myself totally to Him then?"

Instead of rushing foolishly into a marriage because of impatience or one day looking back at our season of singleness with regret, let's commit to using our singleness to its fullest potential. Singleness is a gift. Let's rejoice in it and enjoy its opportunities today. Let's practice trusting God by pursuing His kingdom and His righteousness with all our hearts and by leaving the planning to Him.

In this life we will not understand all He does. But we know that in the end His perfect timing will be revealed. In a poem titled "Sometime," May Riley Smith beautifully expresses the perspective of heaven we will one day possess:

> Sometime, when all life's lessons have been learned,
>   And sun and stars forevermore have set,
> The things which our weak judgments here have spurned,
>   The things o'er which we grieved with lashes wet,
> Will flash before us out of life's dark night,
>   As stars shine most in deeper tints of blue;
> And we shall see how all God's plans are right,
>   And how what seemed reproof was love most true.
> Then be content poor heart;
>   God's plans, like lilies pure and white, unfold;
>   we must not tear the close-shut leaves apart,—

Time will reveal the chalices of gold.
      And if, through patient toil, we reach the land
Where tired feet, with sandals loosed, may rest,
      When we shall clearly see and understand,
I think that we will say, "God knew the best!"

Do you believe that God knows best? Then place your life's calendar at His feet and allow Him to handle the scheduling of your
relationships. Trust Him even if it means not dating when other
people think you should. When God knows you're ready for the
responsibility of commitment, He'll reveal the right person under the
right circumstances.

"For I know the plans I have for you," God says, "plans to pros-
per you and not to harm you, plans to give you hope and a future"
(Jeremiah 29:11). Let's live our *todays* for His kingdom and entrust
our *tomorrows* to His providence.

We couldn't lay our futures in better hands. All we have to do is
trust.

CHAPTER SEVEN

The Direction of Purity

How to Get on the Road to Righteousness

In HIGH SCHOOL I attended a weekend church retreat in which we discussed the topic of sexual purity. During one session our pastor asked all of us to anonymously fill out survey cards that would let him know "how far" kids in the group had gone physically. He provided a rough scale for us to use, assigning numbers to levels of physical intimacy based on their seriousness. The activities ranged from light kissing at number one to sexual intercourse at number ten. Our pastor asked us to write down the highest number we had reached.

After dropping my card into a basket, I filed out of the classroom with two friends. I'll never forget the ensuing conversation. One of my buddies looked over at the other and said with a wink, "So how high did you score?"

Laughing, my other friend said he had reached eight, almost nine. Then these two guys proceeded to name the particular girls in the youth group with whom they had reached certain numbers.

Flirting with Darkness

My two friends exemplify how clouded our understanding of purity has become these days. We esteem purity too little and desire it too late. Even when we try to assert its importance, we render our words meaningless by our contradictory actions.

Do we desire purity in our relationships? We say we do. But do we live lives that foster this purity? Unfortunately, not often enough. "Make me chaste," prayed Augustine, "but not yet." Like him, we often have pricked consciences but unchanged lives. If we were honest with ourselves, many of us would admit that we're not really interested in purity at all. Instead, we feel satisfied by meeting the minimum requirements, content with spending our time in the "gray areas," flirting with darkness and never daring to step into the light of righteousness.

Like countless Christians, my two friends foolishly viewed purity and impurity as separated by a fixed point. As long as they didn't cross the line and go *all the way,* they believed they were still pure. True purity, however, is a direction, a persistent, determined pursuit of righteousness. This direction starts in the heart, and we express it in a lifestyle that flees opportunities for compromise.

One Little Step at a Time

If we truly seek to live pure lives, we can't allow ourselves to detour for even a second from the pursuit of righteousness. A story from the life of King David shows how dangerous such a detour can be. Few stories in the Bible fill me with as much dread as the story of David's fall into sin with Bathsheba. If a righteous man like David could fall into adultery and murder, who on earth can claim to be safe from temptation?

David walked in an intimacy of communion with God that few have known. As a shepherd boy and as the king of God's people, he wrote the Psalms—praises and petitions that encourage and inspire Christians to this day. David reveled in his Creator, worshiped Him, trusted Him, and enjoyed Him. God Himself called David a "man after my own heart" (Acts 13:22).

How could a man with such credentials descend so deep into sin and impurity?

One little step at a time.

David's plunge into sin didn't occur in a single leap. Like every journey into sin, David's journey into iniquity began with an almost imperceptible movement *away* from God.

When we first notice David's slide toward sin, we see him on the rooftop of his palace, but he had created the context for his misstep through an earlier decision. It was the spring of the new year, when kings led their armies to battle. But this year, David didn't go to the battlefield with his army. Instead, he stayed home. The choice may have been trivial, even justifiable, but the fact is that David was not where he was *supposed to be*—he was not on the front lines fighting God's battles.

Was this sin? Not blatantly, but it was a small step away from God's plan.

You may have heard people say that idle hands are the devil's workshop, and so it was for David. The energy he should have exerted on the battlefield needed an outlet. Restless, he paced the palace rooftop. From there he caught sight of a woman bathing. Instead of averting his gaze, he indulged his desires and looked.

Another step.

Why did he continue to watch? He had seen the female body before, having married many times. But he coveted. Sin came in the form of a thought—David desired that which did not belong to him. Instead of rejecting the vileness of this thought, he entertained it, letting it linger in his mind.

If you're like every other human being, you've faced such a moment as this. Dwelling on the pros and cons of bowing to temptation, you have to make a choice. Will you or will you not stay within God's clear boundaries?

At this point in David's story, he could have stopped his journey toward sin. Instead, his hesitating steps down the path quickened into a run. He allowed lust to take control. David acted on his wicked imaginings, sent for Bathsheba, and slept with her.

The innocent shepherd was now an adulterer.

Complications arose. Bathsheba sent a message that she was pregnant. Her husband had been away from home for some time—he could not have fathered the child. Surely Bathsheba's husband, and perhaps the whole nation, would discover her and David's illicit affair. In haste and panic, David attempted to cover up the sin, but his attempts failed. Fearing certain scandal, David signed a letter that sealed the death of Bathsheba's husband, one of David's most loyal soldiers.

The psalmist was now a murderer.

How did David, this man after God's own heart, become an adulterer and murderer? When did he cross the line of purity? Was it the moment he touched Bathsheba or when he kissed her? Did it happen the moment he saw her bathing and chose to watch instead of turn away? Where did purity end and impurity begin?

As you can see from David's story, impurity isn't something we step into suddenly. It happens when we lose our focus on God. Often in dating relationships, impurity starts long before the moments of passion in backseats. Instead it begins in our hearts, in our motivations and attitudes. "I tell you that anyone who looks at a woman lustfully has already committed adultery with her in his heart," Jesus plainly states (Matthew 5:28). Sin begins in our minds and hearts.

We have to understand purity as a *pursuit* of righteousness. When we view it merely as a line not to cross, what keeps us from going as close as we can to the edge? If sex is the line, what's the difference between holding someone's hand and making out with that person? If kissing is the line, what's the difference between a good-night peck and fifteen minutes of passionate liplocking?

If we truly want to pursue purity, then we need to point ourselves in God's direction. We cannot simultaneously explore the boundaries of purity and pursue righteousness—they point us in opposite directions. True purity flees as fast and as far as it can from sin and compromise.

Heart and Path

If we want to lead pure lives, then we must realize that purity does not happen by accident. Rather, we must constantly pursue the direction of purity. The book of Proverbs shows us that this ongoing process involves two things—our hearts and our feet.

In the book of Proverbs, the seductive spirit of impurity and compromise is symbolized by a wayward adulteress. We are warned that "Many are the victims she has brought down; her slain are a mighty throng" (7:26). Though King Solomon wrote these words hundreds of years ago, this "woman" continues to lurk all around us today. She snares the innocent with promises of pleasure, but she truly desires nothing but her victims' destruction. She has ruined countless lives—both male and female—with her treachery.

Throughout history she has crippled the righteous. "Her house," the Bible solemnly warns, "is a highway to the grave, leading down to the chambers of death" (7:27). No matter how "good" impurity's victims may be, or how holy they've been in the past, if they set foot in her house, they speed toward death on an expressway with no exits. Have you ever made a wrong turn onto a freeway only to find that you must travel many miles before you can get off to turn around? If so, you've probably felt the aggravation of your mistake. You can't slow down; you can't turn around; you can only continue speeding farther and farther from your destination. How many Christians in dating relationships have felt the same way as they struggle with accelerating physical involvement? They want to exit, but their own sinful passion takes them further and further from God's will.

How do you avoid the "on-ramp" of impurity? How do you escape the spirit of adultery? Here's the answer: "Do not let your heart turn to her ways or stray into her paths" (7:25). Living a pure life before God requires the teamwork of your heart and your feet. The direction of purity begins within; you must support it in the practical, everyday decisions of where, when, and with whom you choose to be.

Resolve isn't enough by itself. Many people make commitments to sexual purity, but instead of adopting a lifestyle that supports this commitment, they continue relationships that encourage physical expression and place themselves in dangerous settings. "I dated a lot over twenty years ago," a mother of four told me in a letter. "Before my dates I would read my Bible and pray earnestly that I could resist temptation. It didn't work."

It never does. The path you take with your feet should never contradict the conviction of your heart.

Purity in Action

If we desire purity, we have to fight for it. This means adjusting our attitudes and changing our lifestyles. The following pointers will help us maintain a direction of purity with our hearts and our feet.

1. RESPECT THE DEEP SIGNIFICANCE OF PHYSICAL INTIMACY.

We will never understand God's demand for sexual purity until we appreciate the deep spiritual and emotional implications of physical intimacy.

A phone interview I did with a secular radio station in Florida was a reminder for me of the very low view many people have of sex. The dee-jay at this Top 40 rock station and his female cohost (I'll call them Taylor and Crystal) evidently thought an interview with a guy who wasn't having sex would be good for a few laughs. The questions came rapid-fire:

> Taylor: So how old are you?
> Josh: Twenty-three.
> Taylor: Are you a virgin?
> Josh: I am a virgin. Virginal with a capital *V*.
> Taylor: Are you okay?
> Josh: I suppose you're from the school of thought that says if you don't have sex you blow up?
> Taylor: Yeah, it happened to my brother...all over the kitchen.

Crystal: Oh, that's disgusting! Ha, ha…

Taylor: So what's going to happen when, let's say, you get married and you get to the honeymoon suite and she's lousy in bed?

Josh: Well, I won't have anything to compare it to.

(Pause)

Crystal: Now that is a *good* answer!

Josh: I think part of our problem today is that we've reduced sex to some sort of sport. We need manuals and color-coded charts. Instead of being an expression of the intimacy and commitment of a husband and wife, it's all about performing. I think that's part of the reason there's so much sexual dysfunction today—people are terrified that they won't live up to Hollywood's definition of the perfect lover.

Taylor: Yeah, but what if she's lousy in bed, I mean, she just does everything wrong?

Josh: That won't be why I marry her. Do you see the problem with what you're saying? What happens if you marry someone because they're great in bed but then one day they aren't?

Taylor: Cheat!

Josh: Well, sadly that's what some people do.

Crystal: Today we have Taylor being the typical jerk and Josh representing kind, sensitive males.

Josh: But you see, I believe this not because I think it's the "nice thing to do," but because it's what God wants.

What I hope you see is not that Taylor was a jerk and I was a nice, "sensitive guy," as Crystal put it. Like Taylor, many non-Christians view sex as a bodily function on the level of scratching another person's back. They engage in sex whenever and with whomever they want. Although that kind of lifestyle is an affront to biblical values, many Christians treat lesser expressions of physical intimacy with the same lack of respect. They view kissing, holding, or fondling another person as no big deal. We may hold higher standards than our pagan neighbors, but I'm afraid we, too, have lost sight of the deeper significance of sexual intimacy.

"Men tend to see the physical as more of an experience," a good female friend once told me. A girl's point of view is very different, she explained. "Kissing and 'making out' mean something very precious and deep to a woman," she said. "It is our way of giving our trust, our love, our heart to the man we love. It leaves us very vulnerable."

Physical intimacy is much more than two bodies colliding. God designed our sexuality as a physical expression of the oneness of marriage. God guards it carefully and places many stipulations on it because He considers it extremely precious. A man and woman who commit their lives to each other in marriage gain the *right* to express themselves sexually to each other. A husband and wife may enjoy each other's bodies because they in essence belong to each other. But if you're not married to someone, you have no claim on that person's body, no right to sexual intimacy.

Maybe you agree with this and plan to save sex for marriage, yet you view "make-out" activities such as kissing, necking, and sexual touching as no big deal. We need to ask ourselves a serious question: If another person's body doesn't belong to us (that is, we're not married), what right do we have to treat that person any differently than a married person would treat someone who wasn't his or her spouse?

"But," you might say, "that's completely different." Is it really? Our culture has programmed us to think that singleness grants us license to fool around, to try out people emotionally and sexually. Since we're not married to anyone in particular, we can do what we want with anyone in general.

God has a very different view. "Honor marriage, and guard the sacredness of sexual intimacy between wife and husband," He commands (Hebrews 13:4, *The Message*).

This honor for the sacredness of sexuality between husband and wife starts *now*, not just after the wedding day. Respect for the institution of marriage should motivate us to protect it from violation while we're single. We can do this by recognizing the deep significance of sexual intimacy—at *any* level—and refusing to steal these privileges before marriage.

2. SET YOUR STANDARDS TOO HIGH.

In the early days of his ministry, Billy Graham experienced deep concern over the public's distrust of evangelists. How could he preach the gospel to people who assumed he was a fake? As he considered this question, he realized that most people who distrusted evangelists did so because those evangelists lacked integrity, particularly in the area of sexuality. To combat this, he and the close circle of men who ran the crusades avoided opportunities to be alone with women who weren't their wives.

Think about this for a moment. What an inconvenience! Did these men really fear that they'd commit adultery the moment they found themselves alone with a woman? Weren't they going a little too far?

We'll let history answer the question for us. In the last fifty years, what has shaken and demoralized the church as much as the immorality of Christian leaders? What believer can hold his head high when the scandalous conduct of many televangelists is mentioned? But even unbelievers honor the name of Billy Graham. Mr. Graham has earned the respect of the world by his faithfulness and his integrity. How did Billy Graham do this when so many others failed? He set his standards too high—he went above and beyond the call of righteousness.

We can only attain righteousness by doing two things—destroying sin in its embryonic stage and fleeing temptation. Mr. Graham did both. He cut off the opportunity for sin at its root, and he fled from even the possibility of compromise.

God calls us to the same zeal for righteousness in premarital relationships. What exactly does that look like? For me and many other people I know, it has meant rejecting typical dating. I go out with groups of friends; I avoid one-on-one dating because it encourages physical intimacy and places me in an isolated setting with a girl. Can't I handle it? Don't I have any self-control? Yeah, maybe I could handle it, but that's not the point. God says, "Flee the evil desires of youth, and pursue righteousness, faith, love and peace, along with those who call on the Lord out of a pure heart" (2 Timothy 2:22). I won't stick around to see how much temptation I can take. God is not impressed with my ability to stand up to sin. He's more impressed by the obedience I show when I run from it.

For couples moving toward engagement or those already engaged, the same principle applies. Set your standards higher than you need to. Cut off sin at its root. Until you're married—and I mean until you've walked down that aisle and exchanged vows—don't act as if your bodies belong to each other.

Maybe you think I'm taking this idea too far. Maybe you're saying, "You've got to be joking. One little kiss won't have me hurtling toward certain sin." Let me encourage you to give this idea a little more thought. For just a moment, consider the possibility that even the most innocent form of sexual expression outside of marriage could be dangerous.

Let me explain why I believe this. Physical interaction encourages us to start something we're not supposed to finish, awakening desires we're not allowed to consummate, turning on passions we have to turn off. What foolishness! The Bible tells us that the path of sin, particularly in regard to the wrong use of our sexuality, is like a highway to the grave. We shouldn't get on it then try to stop before we arrive at the destination—God tells us to stay off that highway completely.

In an e-mail, seventeen-year-old Mandi told me the sad story of how her once "very high standards" were steadily eroded by her boyfriend. Mandi came from a strong Christian home, was active in her youth group and planned to be a virgin on her wedding night. But "little things" like extra-long hugs, hand-holding, and kisses on the cheek wore down her resolve. "I didn't realize how 'just kissing' brings on tons of other emotions that I never knew existed," she told me. "Two days before our two-year anniversary I finally gave in, and I lost my virginity. The shame that covered me was indescribable," she recounted. "Later on that day I took a shower and scrubbed my entire body a million times, thinking this would make me feel clean. It only left some red marks that my tears blinded me from noticing."

God designed our sexuality to operate within the protection and commitment of marriage. God made sex to end in full consummation. Every step along the path of pure sexuality—from an initial glance between husband and wife, to a kiss—potentially leads toward physical oneness. In marriage, things are supposed to progress—things are *allowed* to get "out of hand."

And I really believe that before marriage we can't keep from abusing God's gift of sex unless we choose to stay off the path altogether. In Colossians 3:5 we read, "Put to death, therefore, whatever belongs to your earthly nature: sexual immorality, impurity, lust, evil desires." Tolerated sin is pampered sin—it grows and gains strength. James tells us that "each one is tempted when, by his own evil desire, he is dragged away and enticed. Then, after desire has conceived, it gives birth to sin; and sin, when it is full-grown, gives birth to death" (1:14–15). If we begin the progression of sin and allow it to continue, it will soon grow beyond our control. Only by keeping our standards too high and killing sin in its infantile stage will we avoid its destruction.

Set your standards too high. You will never regret purity.

3. MAKE THE PURITY OF OTHERS A PRIORITY.

One of the best ways to maintain a pure life is to watch out for the purity of others. What can you do to protect your brothers and sisters in the Lord from impurity? What can you say to encourage them to keep their hearts set in the direction of righteousness?

The support and protection you can provide to same-sex friends is important, but the protection you can give to opposite-sex friends is invaluable. When it comes to purity in relationships—both physical and emotional—girls and guys usually trip each other up. Can you imagine the righteousness that could be born if both sexes took it upon themselves to watch out for each other?

Let's look at specific ways this can be accomplished.

The Guy's Responsibility

Guys, it's time we stood up to defend the honor and righteousness of our sisters. We need to stop acting like hunters trying to catch girls and begin seeing ourselves as warriors standing guard over them.

How do we do this? First we must realize that girls don't struggle with the same temptations we struggle with. We wrestle more with our sex drives, while girls struggle more with their emotions. We can help guard their hearts by being sincere and honest in our communication. We need to swear off flirtatiousness and refuse to play games and lead them on. We have to go out of our way to make sure nothing we say or do stirs up inappropriate feelings or expectations.

A good friend, Matt Canlis, modeled this idea of guarding a girl's purity in his relationship with Julie Clifton, the woman to whom he's now married. Long before they began pursuing marriage, both felt deeply attracted to the other. But during a certain season, God made it clear to Julie that she had to focus on Him and not be distracted by Matt.

Although Matt didn't know this at the time, he made it his priority to guard Julie's heart during this time of waiting, even though he felt personally drawn to her. Matt controlled his desire to flirt with Julie. He passed up opportunities to spend time alone with her, and when they were in group settings he refrained from singling her out and focusing too much attention on her. He avoided doing anything that would make it harder for Julie to focus on serving God.

This season didn't last forever, and eventually Matt and Julie became engaged. I had lunch with both of them a few weeks before their wedding. Julie explained how grateful she felt that Matt had enough maturity to put her needs above his own. By making her emotional and spiritual purity a priority, Matt helped Julie focus her mind and heart on God. If Matt had acted selfishly, he could have distracted Julie from what God wanted to accomplish in and through her life.

What an example of brotherly love! I want to weep when I think of the many times I have neglected my responsibility to guard girls' hearts. Instead of playing the role of a warrior, I played the thief, stealing their focus from God for myself. I'm determined to do better. I want to be the kind of friend to whom girls' future husbands could one day say, "Thank you for standing watch over my wife's heart. Thank you for guarding her purity."

The Girl's Responsibility

Girls, you have an equally important role. Remember the wayward woman we discussed earlier? Your job is to keep your brothers from being led astray by her charms. Please be aware of how easily your actions and glances can stir up lust in a guy's mind.

You may not realize this, but we guys most commonly struggle with our eyes. I think many girls are innocently unaware of the difficulty a guy has in remaining pure when looking at a girl who is dressed immodestly. Now, I don't want to dictate your wardrobe, but honestly speaking, I would be blessed if girls considered more than fashion when shopping for clothes. Yes, guys are responsible for maintaining self-control, but you can help by refusing to wear clothing designed to attract attention to your body.

I know the world tells you that if you have a nice body, you should show it off. And we men have only helped feed this mentality. But I think you can play a part in reversing this trend. A single mom who had recently rededicated her life to Christ told me, "I went through my closet and got rid of anything that might have caused a brother in the Lord to stumble. I asked God to forgive me and to help me protect the purity of those around me." Aly from Wisconsin wrote, "I think I'll have to get rid of over half my wardrobe, because much of what I have is too revealing or tempts men to look at me and think impure thoughts."

Are you willing to be that radical? My friend Janelle asks her dad to evaluate every outfit she buys. She wants a godly man's opinion of whether or not it's modest. It's not always easy. There have been many times her dad has asked her to return items. But she doesn't complain—even in the summer, when it seems impossible to find a modest pair of shorts! She wants to honor God.

I know many girls who would look great in shorter skirts or

tighter blouses, and they know it. But they choose to dress modestly. They take the responsibility of guarding their brothers' eyes. To these women and others like them, I'm grateful.

"And let us consider how we may spur one another on toward love and good deeds" (Hebrews 10:24). It's time to start seeing other people's purity as our responsibility.

The Beauty of Purity

In closing, let me ask you this: Can you picture it? Can you see the beauty of purity? And if you can, will you fight for it in your own life as well as in the lives of others?

Yes, it requires work. Purity doesn't happen by accident; it requires obedience to God. But this obedience is not burdensome or overbearing. We have only to consider the alternatives to impurity to see the beauty of walking in God's will. Impurity is a grimy film that coats the soul, a shadow that blocks light and darkens our countenance. God's love for the impure does not cease, but their ability to enjoy this love does. For in our impurity we are turned from Him. Sin and its defilement are never found near His throne—they can only gain advantage when we turn away from His radiance.

Turned from God's presence we are completely unprotected from the marauding destruction of sin. Without purity, God's gift of sexuality becomes a dangerous game. A relationship devoid of purity is soon reduced to nothing more than two bodies grasping at and demanding pleasure. Without purity, the mind becomes a slave to depravity, tossed about by every sinful craving and imagination.

What will it take for us to see the beauty of purity? Purity is the entrance to the splendor of God's creation. "Who may ascend the hill of the LORD? Who may stand in his holy place? He who has clean hands and a pure heart" (Psalm 24:3–4). Purity ushers us into God's presence. "Blessed are the pure in heart," Christ said, "for they will see God" (Matthew 5:8). Only the pure may see His face. Only the pure may be vessels of His Holy Spirit.

Do you see the beauty and power and protection of purity? Do you want all this? Do you ache for it? Are you ready to deny yourself the pleasures of the moment to live a pure, God-focused life? May your love for Him fuel a lifelong, passionate pursuit of righteousness.

CHAPTER EIGHT

A Cleansed Past:
The Room

How Jesus Can Redeem Your Past

I DON'T USUALLY SHARE my dreams with people, but I'd like to tell you about a particularly stirring one I once had.

As Christians, we "know" certain things such as "Jesus loves me" and "Christ died for sinners." We've heard these statements countless times, but the dust of familiarity can dim the glory of these simple truths. We have to brush them off and remind ourselves of their life-transforming power.

A dream I had one humid night while visiting a pastor in Puerto Rico was one such reminder. It summed up what Jesus Christ did for me and for you.

I share it here because after a chapter on the importance of striving for purity, we need a reminder of God's grace. For some, myself included, a discussion of purity is an exercise in regret—it reminds us of our impurity and the times we've failed.

Maybe you've blown it. Maybe you reflect on past actions and wince with remorse. Purity seems like a lost cause. This dream, called "The Room," is dedicated to you.

103

ᴖᴗ

In that place between wakefulness and dreams, I found myself in the room. There were no distinguishing features save for the one wall covered with small index-card files.

They were like the ones in libraries that list titles by author or subject in alphabetical order. But these files, which stretched from floor to ceiling and seemingly endlessly in either direction, had very different headings. As I drew near the wall of files, the first to catch my attention was one that read "Girls I Have Liked." I opened it and began flipping through the cards. I quickly shut it, shocked to realize that I recognized the names written on each one.

And then without being told, I knew exactly where I was. This lifeless room with its small files was a crude catalog system for my life. Here were written the actions of my every moment, big and small, in a detail my memory couldn't match.

A sense of wonder and curiosity, coupled with horror, stirred within me as I began randomly opening files and exploring their contents. Some brought joy and sweet memories; others a sense of shame and regret so intense that I would look over my shoulder to see if anyone was watching. A file named "Friends" was next to one marked "Friends I Have Betrayed."

The titles ranged from the mundane to the outright weird: "Books I Have Read," "Lies I Have Told," "Comfort I Have Given," "Jokes I Have Laughed At." Some were almost hilarious in their exactness: "Things I've Yelled at My Brothers." Others I couldn't laugh at: "Things I Have Done in Anger," "Things I Have Muttered under My Breath at My Parents." I never ceased to be surprised by the contents. Often there were many more cards than I expected. Sometimes there were fewer than I hoped.

I was overwhelmed by the sheer volume of the life I had

lived. Could it be possible that I had the time in my twenty years to write each of these thousands, possibly millions, of cards? But each card confirmed this truth. Each was written in my own handwriting. Each signed with my signature.

When I pulled out the file marked "Songs I Have Listened To," I realized the files grew to contain their contents. The cards were packed tightly, and yet after two or three yards, I hadn't found the end of the file. I shut it, shamed, not so much by the quality of music, but more by the vast amount of time I knew that file represented.

When I came to a file marked "Lustful Thoughts," I felt a chill run through my body. I pulled the file out only an inch, not willing to test its size, and drew out a card. I shuddered at its detailed contents. I felt sick to think that such a moment had been recorded.

Suddenly I felt an almost animal rage. One thought dominated my mind: "No one must ever see these cards! No one must ever see this room! I have to destroy them!" In an insane frenzy I yanked the file out. Its size didn't matter now. I had to empty it and burn the cards. But as I took the file at one end and began pounding it on the floor, I could not dislodge a single card. I became desperate and pulled out a card, only to find it as strong as steel when I tried to tear it.

Defeated and utterly helpless, I returned the file to its slot. Leaning my forehead against the wall, I let out a long, self-pitying sigh. And then I saw it. The title bore "People I Have Shared the Gospel With." The handle was brighter than those around it, newer, almost unused. I pulled on its handle and a small box not more than three inches long fell into my hands. I could count the cards it contained on one hand.

And then the tears came. I began to weep. Sobs so deep that the hurt started in my stomach and shook through me. I fell on my knees and cried. I cried out of shame, from the overwhelming shame of it all. The rows of file shelves swirled in my tear-filled eyes. No one must ever, ever know of this room. I must lock it up and hide the key.

But then as I pushed away the tears, I saw Him. *No, please, not Him. Not here. Oh, anyone but Jesus.*

I watched helplessly as He began to open the files and read the cards. I couldn't bear to watch His response. And in the moments I could bring myself to look at His face, I saw a sorrow deeper than my own. He seemed to intuitively go to the worst boxes. Why did He have to read every one?

Finally He turned and looked at me from across the room. He looked at me with pity in His eyes. But this was a pity that didn't anger me. I dropped my head, covered my face with my hands, and began to cry again. He walked over and put His arm around me. He could have said so many things. But He didn't say a word. He just cried with me.

Then He got up and walked back to the wall of files. Starting at one end of the room, He took out a file and, one by one, began to sign His name over mine on each card.

"No!" I shouted, rushing to Him. All I could find to say was "No, no," as I pulled the card from Him. His name shouldn't be on these cards. But there it was, written in red so rich, so dark, so alive. The name of Jesus covered mine. It was written with His blood.

He gently took the card back. He smiled a sad smile and continued to sign the cards. I don't think I'll ever understand how He did it so quickly, but the next instant it seemed I heard Him close the last file and walk back to my side. He placed His hand on my shoulder and said, "It is finished."

I stood up, and He led me out of the room. There was no lock on its door. There were still cards to be written.

More than a Nice Story

I originally shared the story of my dream back in 1995 in a magazine I published. Since then it's been e-mailed and spread by many people—

even by those who aren't Christians. For some no doubt it's a nice story, and though it isn't real to them, its religious overtones and theme of forgiveness makes them feel good.

But this is more than a heart-warming story. It's not imaginary. The dream is a picture of what Christ truly accomplished when He died on the cross. He literally took our guilt on Himself. And this meant much more than just having His name on a card. It meant receiving the punishment from God that all those sinful words and actions deserved.

Here is what's important to understand: It is only by repenting of our sins and putting our faith in Christ that this substitution can take place. We each have a "room" containing all our sinful deeds and thoughts. But just because we admit this or feel bad about it doesn't mean we're forgiven. Remorse can't save anyone. Only faith in Christ can. Only trust in His death and resurrection for us.

Whose Name Is on Your Cards?

The Bible teaches that one day we'll each stand before God to be judged. "So then, each of us will give an account of himself to God" (Romans 14:12). All the "cards" from our life will be dumped out before Him for review.

The hope I have for that day isn't that I've written enough good cards to make up for the bad. My hope for that day is in the fact that I've put my faith in God's perfect Son. He has already paid the penalty for my sin. Even though I deserve to be punished, even though I'm guilty, the name of Jesus will be on those cards.

For sinners like you and me, there's no better news. We can be forgiven. Every man and woman who believes on Jesus can be cleansed—no matter how dark the stain of sin.

"So let us put aside the deeds of darkness and put on the armor of light" (Romans 13:12). Admittedly, some will have more to lay aside than others—more memories, more pain, more regrets. But the past needn't determine our future. We have choices right now about how we'll live. Will we set our hearts on God and walk in His paths?

"Let us behave decently," the passage in Romans continues, "...not in sexual immorality and debauchery.... Rather, clothe yourselves with the Lord Jesus Christ, and do not think about how to gratify the desires of the sinful nature" (vv. 13–14).

Not one of us can stand completely pure before God. We are all sinners. But no matter how filthy the rags of our defilement may be, in a moment of repentance and faith the heart turned toward God loses its impurity. God clothes us in Christ's righteousness. He no longer sees our sin. He transfers Jesus' purity to us. So see yourself as God sees you—clothed in radiant white, pure, justified.

Maybe you have a particular memory that continues to hound you, a memory that makes you feel unworthy of God's love and forgiveness.

Turn away from it. Don't replay that moment or any others like it. If you've rejected all those behaviors, God has promised to remember them no more (Hebrews 8:12). Move on. A lifetime of purity awaits you.

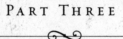

PART THREE

Building a
New Lifestyle

CHAPTER NINE

Starting with a Clean Slate

Five Important Steps for Getting on Track with God's Plan

Building well sometimes means first tearing down.

Recently my dad and my younger brother Joel attended a birthday party for Stephen Taylor, one of Joel's best friends. It was a very special occasion. Stephen was turning thirteen, and his dad wanted to make Stephen's entrance into young adulthood memorable. Nice presents wouldn't suffice; Stephen's dad wanted to impart wisdom. To accomplish this he asked fathers to come with their sons to the party and to bring a special gift—a tool that served them in their specific lines of work.

Each father gave his tool to Stephen along with its accompanying life lesson for the "toolbox" of principles Stephen would carry into life. The tools were as unique as the men who used them. My dad gave Stephen a quality writing pen and explained that a pen not only served him when he wrote his ideas but also represented his word when he signed an agreement.

During the gift giving, a father who was a professional home builder handed Stephen a small box. "Inside that box is the tool I use most," he said. Stephen opened it and found a nail puller.

"My nail puller, simple as it might seem," the father explained, "is one of the most important tools I have." This father told the story of how once, while in the middle of building a wall, he discovered that it was crooked. Instead of halting the construction and undoing a little work to fix the wall, he decided to proceed, hoping that the problem would go away as he continued to build. However, the problem only worsened. Eventually, at a great loss of materials and time, he had to tear down the nearly completed wall and totally rebuild it.

"Stephen," the father said gravely, "times will come in life when you realize you've made a mistake. At that moment, you have two choices: You can swallow your pride and 'pull a few nails,' or you can foolishly continue your course, hoping the problem will go away. Most of the time the problem will only get worse. I'm giving you this tool to remind you of this principle: When you realize you've made a mistake, the best thing you can do is tear down the wall and start over."

Building a Godly Lifestyle

The lesson of the nail puller is an important one for all of us who have built our relationships on the faulty attitudes and patterns of this world. For many, getting things right will require us to first tear down what's wrong. In some cases, that means bringing wrong relationships to an end.

Whatever your circumstances, the following steps are important for starting and maintaining a lifestyle of godliness in relationships.

1. START WITH A CLEAN SLATE.

If we want to build a godly lifestyle, we must first repent of sinful attitudes and behaviors in our relationships. The Bible uses the word *repent* to describe turning from what's wrong and pursuing what's right. Repentance is a change of direction based on a change of heart.

There's a difference between a true change of heart and merely feeling sorry because of the consequences of sin. Once, after preaching at a Christian music festival, I was approached in the prayer tent by Emily and her three friends. With a giggle that contradicted her words, Emily told me she kept "messing up" with boys and wanted God to help her change. As I asked her additional questions, it became clear that Emily wasn't actually convicted of her sin. She didn't like the consequences of losing her virginity or of having guys break up with her, but there was no sadness over disobeying and failing to honor God.

In 2 Corinthians 7:10, Paul contrasts godly sorrow with the brand of worldly sorrow Emily modeled. "Godly sorrow brings repentance that leads to salvation and leaves no regret, but worldly sorrow brings death."

Worldly sorrow is self-centered and leads to shame, but not to change. Godly sorrow recognizes sin as an offense against God, turns to Christ for forgiveness, and leads to a transformed life. This is what it means to truly "clean the slate" and start afresh.

Have you practiced selfishness in relationships? Admit your selfishness and correct it. Have you played fast and loose in the area of purity? Then cultivate genuine, godly sorrow, and ask God to forgive then reverse your sinful course. Are you currently involved in a relationship that you know is wrong? Then ask God to give you the courage to do His will, which might include breaking off the relationship.

Breaking Up Is Hard to Do

Danny, an eighteen-year-old, knew that he could fix the problems in his relationship with Trisha by doing only one thing: ending the relationship. They had dated for over seven months, and during that time, they had quickly escalated their physical involvement. They didn't mean to, but no matter how many times they made rules about where to stop, they always went further. Neither was ready to get married, and deep down Danny really didn't believe he and Trisha were right for each other anyway. Continuing the relationship with Trisha would only mislead her.

Did any of these factors make breaking up easy? No, this messy aspect of relationships will always be hard. But remember, continuing a wrong relationship only increases the pain when it finally does end. Have the courage to obey now. Obedience today will save you a lot of sorrow and regret tomorrow.

When you end a relationship, you need to remember a couple of important things. First, really end it. Don't leave any strings attached or hint at the possibility of reuniting someday. You should also probably agree to steer clear of each other for a while afterward. In Danny's case, he felt tempted to call Trisha after their breakup "just to chat" or to ask her to go out "just for old time's sake." But doing so would only reawaken old feelings. Though it wasn't easy, he knew that he and Trisha had to end the relationship with finality.

Adjusting the Focus of a Relationship

One day Sheena realized that a relationship with one of her guy friends from church was becoming more and more serious. They weren't dating, but they always seemed to end up together in groups, and they talked on the phone quite often. Upon realizing this, Sheena decided to sit down with her friend and express her concern: "I really want to be friends with you, but I think we focus a little too much time on each other." Though Sheena struggled to muster the nerve to say this, that little conversation helped keep the friendship on the right track.

Starting with a clean slate doesn't always involve a breakup. Sometimes it simply means refocusing a relationship to keep it from heading in the wrong direction.

No Blame Shifting

When Jonathan broke up with Kara, he didn't try to point out how she shared the blame for problems in their relationship. "That wouldn't have been apologizing," he said. Instead, he asked her to forgive him for being the one to push the physical side of their relationship. "I told her I'd been a terrible example of a Christian and that ending the relationship was what I believed God wanted me to do."

Whether you're having to break up or refocus a relationship, approach the other person humbly, stressing your desire to please God. Remember, you don't have to prove them wrong to do what you know is right. There's a good chance they won't understand at first or will think you're making up an excuse for bringing the relationship to an end. Don't try to argue with them or prove a point.

If you've wronged that person, confess your guilt and ask for forgiveness. Don't rationalize or make excuses. Just apologize.

2. Make your parents your teammates.

You'll need two things as you live out a new attitude toward relationships: wisdom and accountability. Ideally, both of these should come from your parents. You need your mom and dad. (I realize that not everyone has the opportunity to benefit from relationships with both parents, but even so, I believe that you can gain valuable insight from whichever parent or guardian you most trust.)

Why do I say we need to gain wisdom and accountability from our parents? Because I can see how I shot myself in the foot in the past by *not* trusting my parents. When I was in junior high and high school, I hid my relationships from my parents. If I liked someone, I wouldn't let my parents know. I feared that if they got involved they'd mess things up. What a mistake! By hiding my romantic life from my parents, I cut myself off from a God-given source of wisdom that could have saved me from making so many mistakes.

I've spent the last several years learning to be open and honest with my parents about my romantic interests. And as I've done this, I've made an incredible discovery: *My mom and dad are on my side!* What a relief to tell them what I'm going through! These conversations don't have to be embarrassing or confrontational. I just go to my parents and say, "I've been thinking about so-and-so. What do you guys think of her?" Or "I'm really distracted by this person. Would you pray for me?"

As I openly discuss my thoughts and feelings with my parents, they can remind me of God's Word and the commitments I've made (a pretty girl can so easily make me forget them!). They can also provide prayer and counsel. But they can't do this unless I choose to actively involve them and seek their wisdom. I've gained some wonderful insights as I've done this and I think you could, too. I challenge you to make your parents your teammates.

When Dad and Mom Aren't Around

As I mentioned earlier, I realize that some people just don't have the option to involve their parents in this way. Maybe your parents are divorced, non-Christians, or just uninterested in being involved. Or you may be an older single living away from home.

If you're in one of these situations, please understand that God can provide all the support you need. He does this through His Holy Spirit and through the lives of other Christians in your local church. You need a mentor who will give you wisdom and accountability regarding your relationships. Ask God to show you who to turn to. Then, when He brings a mentor into your life, actively invite that person's input. If you're not already involved in a church, find one and ask a godly older man or woman there to fill the role of adopted dad or mom as you navigate the sea of romantic relationships.

Whatever your circumstances, don't procrastinate. Develop a support team to help you stay on track.

3. ESTABLISH CLEAR GUIDELINES.

After you've formed your "team," you need to establish guidelines for your relationships with the opposite sex that are based on the wisdom of God's Word. Sit down with your mom and dad, or mentor, and ask questions such as "What constitutes a romantic setting? When is going out with someone appropriate, and when would it lead to premature intimacy?" Think through some of the situations that might arise. What do you do when someone feels attracted to you, or vice versa? How much time should you spend on the phone with someone of the opposite sex? How much time should you spend together, even in group settings? There are not hard and fast rules. These are issues of wisdom and will differ based on your age and spiritual maturity.

Setting guidelines like these will allow you to respond with confidence in different situations. For example, I have committed to avoiding situations that could lead to temptation. For me, being alone with a girl in an empty house is one such situation. So I've created a "policy" about this issue: I will not go to a girl's home if no one else is there. If a girl calls me, invites me to come over, and mentions in passing that her parents aren't home, I don't have to weigh the situation or pray about it—I already know that I won't accept the invitation.

Rules by themselves won't change our hearts, but once we've taken on a new attitude, protective guidelines can help keep us on course.

4. CHECK TO SEE WHO'S WHISPERING IN YOUR EAR.

Finally, keep an eye on your influences. Who and what you listen to, read, and watch will either encourage or conflict with your commitment to pursue God's best in relationships.

I remember talking to a girl at my church who commented on how dissatisfied she felt after watching romantic movies. "It makes me wonder, 'Why doesn't that happen to me?'" she said.

Does anything in your life cause that kind of discontentment? If so, then maybe you need to consider cutting out some things. Maybe you need to stop reading romance novels and watching soap operas because they encourage ungodly longings within you. Perhaps you need to turn off the radio because much of today's music exalts a false definition of love. You might need to tune out some of your favorite TV shows because they mock your beliefs about purity. Whatever tempts you toward discontentment or compromise, don't put up with it. Tune it out. Turn it off.

You may find that a similar principle applies to spending too much time with friends who are obsessed with the dating scene. I'm not saying that you should dump your friends because they encourage you to dwell on dating, but I do think you should be aware of how your friends affect your thoughts. Ask yourself these questions: Are these people negatively affecting me? How can I be a positive influence on them without compromising my convictions? The answer might involve spending less time with certain people or choosing to spend time with them in different settings. Pray for these friends and love them, but honestly assess their influence on you. And ask God to bring people into your life who will provide support for your standards and beliefs.

5. SEASON YOUR CONVICTION WITH HUMILITY.

This leads to the question of how to politely explain our convictions about dating with others. How do you decline a date when someone asks you out? One girl e-mailed me, "Help! I've turned down two dates in the last week. I'm running out of excuses!" Or what do you tell your prying relatives when they ask why you don't have a girlfriend? How can you communicate your convictions without coming across as self-righteous or as a hermit?

It requires wisdom and humility to respond appropriately in different situations. I try to keep in mind that my primary purpose for communicating with others should be their encouragement and growth. What this means practically is that sometimes we should explain our convictions and reasons for not dating in detail, and other times we shouldn't. Sometimes our explanations are helpful, protecting others' feelings and possibly even challenging them. But other times our rationale only confuses people, ruining a chance for the natural growth of friendship and sending out a holier-than-thou signal.

Different Answers for Different People

So how do we decide when to share our views with others? It's not an easy call, but we can learn to differentiate between the good and bad times by understanding the two types of relationships in our lives: those that are merely limited acquaintances and those that are established and ongoing.

When I don't feel close to a person, I rarely dive into a discussion about my views on dating. People who don't know me well might misinterpret my statements or think I'm being judgmental. So for example, if a person who is new at church asks me if I'm seeing someone, I smile nicely and say that I'm not in a relationship at the moment. Launching into a discussion of the seven habits of highly defective dating would be overkill.

On the other hand, I do explain my convictions to my close friends. They know I don't want to be "set up" with anyone and that I want only friendships until I'm ready for marriage. I've discussed this with my friends and shared books and articles that have influenced my thinking. Whether or not my friends agree, I've invested the time to explain where I stand. This makes my life much easier and protects their feelings. For example, I once made plans to go to a movie with a group of friends. At the last minute, everyone backed out except for one girl. But because she knew I avoided one-on-one dates with girls, she called to say we'd need to reschedule. Her feelings weren't hurt, and I didn't have to go into a major explanation. She respected and worked with my beliefs.

Don't Try to Win an Argument

When the time comes to share why you don't date, what should you say? Whatever words you use, remember that the goal of your communication is not winning a debate or convincing your hearers of your view. If your friends agree, great! But your main goal is to humbly communicate what you feel God has shown you, to encourage your friends, and to contribute to their growth.

As you explain your stance on dating, make specific statements about your own life, not general statements about everyone else. Remember, it's not your responsibility to live everyone else's life for them, just your own. Focus on what God has spoken to your heart. Be humble and honest about how you're trying to be obedient. If you maintain this humble spirit, you'll often find your listener willing to share his or her own struggles and questions. This opens up the opportunity for you to give counsel and support.

If someone asks you out, make sure he or she understands that you're not rejecting him or her personally or the possibility for friendship. Just make it clear that you're not at a place in your life when you're pursuing anything more than friendship. If this is someone you'd like to get to know better, explain the kinds of settings in which you typically interact with friends of the opposite sex. Invite them along to a group activity.

Our key motive in communicating our beliefs about dating should be to serve others. We want to promote peace, love, and righteousness that will bring glory to God. When we feel overly concerned about people's opinions of us, when we concentrate on proving we're "right," we're likely to become defensive and overbearing. But when we make our top priority showing God's love to others and thinking about their feelings, we'll find it easier to make wise decisions about what we do and do not say.

When you get one of those "You don't date? Are you okay?" looks from people, adopt the apostle Paul's attitude when he described the abuse we suffer for following Christ: "Being reviled, we bless; being persecuted, we endure; being defamed, we entreat" (1 Corinthians 4:12–13, NKJV).

The Bible tells us we're to bear the pain of ridicule without flinching. When you face scorn from people who don't understand your convictions about dating, instead of lashing out, respond with kindness and ask God to show those people the same mercy He has shown you.

Let's Live It

The pastor A. W. Tozer once preached a particularly convicting sermon to his congregation. One person who heard it recalls that, had he so desired, Tozer could have filled the altar with a repentant, sobbing throng. But Tozer wasn't interested in a display of emotion. Instead of delivering an altar call, Tozer told his congregation to quietly leave the service. "Don't come down here and cry about it," he boomed. "Go home and live it!"

Tozer's instruction is perfect for us. Though they might seem difficult at first, the five steps we've examined in this chapter are a vital part of building a new lifestyle. They will not only help us start strong, but even more important, they can help us follow through—to "go home and live" what's right.

We can take our first step by refocusing relationships that are headed off course or ending those we know are wrong. To embrace all the good God has in store for us, we need to repent of past sin. We also need a team—parents and other godly friends—who can keep us accountable and provide encouragement. Let's be humble enough to invite their correction and counsel. And let's be honest enough to admit we need protective guidelines in our lives to keep us far from temptation and compromise. Let's honestly evaluate the influence of what we watch, what we listen to, and who we hang out with. Finally, let's hold our convictions with humility. Actively following the five steps in this chapter will help us put our convictions into action.

Yes, we'll still face many questions. How can we have friendships with the opposite sex without becoming romantic? What do we do when attracted to or even infatuated with someone? And how can we explain "not dating" to those around us? We'll look at these and many other issues in the next three chapters.

CHAPTER TEN

Just Friends in a Just-Do-It World

Keys for Keeping Your Relationships with the Opposite Sex out of the "Romantic Zone"

Y OU MEET SOMEONE of the opposite sex. He or she really catches your eye.

Uh-oh.

Then you get to know this person, and you find out he or she has a great personality as well.

Double uh-oh.

To top it all off, this person sends you that "I'd like to get to know you better" vibe.

Major uh-oh!

If you've decided to put romance on hold until you're ready for marriage, what do you do in a situation like this? If you're not going to play the dating game, what's the plan?

The simple answer is to just be friends. Easy, right? Not quite. Maybe we wouldn't struggle with this scenario if God created us without hearts, devoid of emotions, and immune to attraction. But He didn't. Most of us have to deal with all three as we stumble through the confusing process of finding balance between two extreme options: jumping headlong into romance with everyone who catches our eye or running in fear from all members of the opposite sex. Finding that balance is anything but easy. The middle ground can often feel more like a tightrope stretched over a gaping chasm.

Just Plain Confusing

Being "just friends" is just plain confusing. In all honesty, I haven't completely figured it out. Romance runs in my veins, and it's not always easy to restrain. Even when I want to maintain a platonic relationship with a girl, I struggle to keep myself from stepping into something more.

Where is the line between friendship and "more than friendship," anyway? Trying to answer that question reminds me of a Tootsie Pop commercial I watched as a kid. Maybe you've seen it. A little boy has a Tootsie Pop and a very valid question: How many licks does it take to get to the middle of a Tootsie Roll–filled lollipop?

He asks a couple of animals his question, but nobody knows the answer. They direct him to the owl. The owl would know; owls are smart.

So the boy poses his question to the owl, who sits in his tree like some mountaintop guru: "How many licks does it take to get to the chewy center of a Tootsie Pop?"

The owl thoughtfully takes the sucker and removes the wrapping.

He licks once. "One," he counts.

He licks again. "Two," he says.

He licks a third time. "Three."

And suddenly, *crunch!* Throwing patience to the wind, the owl bites into the middle of the Tootsie Pop. Handing the bare Tootsie Pop stick to the boy, the owl announces his answer to the mystifying question: "Three."

That owl made me so mad when I was a kid. I felt sorry for the boy. Not only did he lose his Tootsie Pop, but he still didn't know the true answer to his question.

When I consider friendship with girls, I feel like that boy! I don't want to reach the chewy center of romance—I just want to be friends. But I don't always know how much attention a friendship between a guy and girl can handle before—*crunch!*—we've crossed the line from friendship into more than friendship.

I don't raise this concern because I'm afraid of romance. On the contrary, I look forward to one day growing to love a girl and doing my best to sweep her off her feet. But until that time comes, I want to focus on serving God in my singleness. To stay on this course, I've chosen to avoid dating, steering clear of any romantic entanglements.

But sometimes my friendships go *crunch*.

Have you ever realized that a friendship has tipped over into romance? If so, then you know how difficult it can be to avoid this situation. One moment you're pals; then all of a sudden your heart kicks into high gear. You sigh when you think of this person. You find yourself daydreaming of the next time you can spend time with this "friend." Or you're with a group of friends, and when that particular person talks with someone else you feel…something. Jealous? Possessive?

You try to reason with yourself. "Why would I feel this way? We're just friends. We're brother and sister in Christ…" You can say whatever you want, but you know deep down that you've *crunched*.

Friends Forever

To my shame, I have a whole file of my own *crunch!* stories—friendships with girls complicated, and sometimes ruined, because we became romantic. I'll share one of these stories here to help show how *crunching* can happen.

At age seventeen, I had just gotten out of a serious, two-year relationship that had shown me firsthand the pitfalls of dating. While my former girlfriend was, and is, a wonderful person, we broke up with many regrets. But now I had a chance to start over, and I was determined to avoid the mistakes of the past. I developed a simple plan: Until I was ready for marriage and had found the right girl, I would just be friends with members of the opposite sex.

Easier said than done.

I had good intentions, but I set out with a naive understanding of the nature of guy-girl friendships. At this point in time, I thought friendship with a girl meant you didn't kiss her or officially date. I had a lot to learn.

With my limited understanding, I embarked on my new approach to friendships with girls. It didn't take long before I had a chance to test my ideas. I met Chelsea the summer before my senior year in high school. She was a fellow student at The Summit, a Christian leadership training camp held in a quaint but rickety turn-of-the-century hotel in Colorado Springs, Colorado. Chelsea and I met on the stairs one day between classes. She was a pretty brunette from Kansas who radiated wholesomeness. A strong Christian from a good family, Chelsea was as American as apple pie—athletic and adventurous. It was definitely a case of "like" at first sight.

Over the course of the camp we got to know each other, talking in the lunch line and playing tennis on sports days. We grew even closer when we and a group of students hiked fourteen miles to the top of Pikes Peak. During the trek, Chelsea told me about life in the small town where her dad practiced law. I told her about my life at home in Oregon. As we talked, I felt elated to have found a girl whose company I could enjoy without all the trappings of being boyfriend and girlfriend.

Unfortunately, my desire for "just friendship" wasn't as strong as my old habits of edging toward romance with girls. I felt attracted to Chelsea, and instead of being content with friendship and keeping our interaction in the context of a group, I asked her out to lunch. She accepted, and two days before camp ended, we rode the bus into downtown Colorado Springs. We spent the afternoon meandering through tourist traps full of knickknacks and cheap paintings. At a bead shop we made necklaces as reminders of each other.

This little date was Mistake Number One. In my opinion, going out to lunch isn't a big deal, but in this case it signaled my special interest in Chelsea, placed us in a romantically charged setting, and made us feel like a couple. My instigation of this interaction pushed our relationship beyond friendship.

But at the time I was blind to all of this. In fact, I felt proud of myself. As far as I was concerned, Chelsea and I had been completely above reproach. Good grief! We hadn't so much as held hands! As "mature" high schoolers, we had risen above the junior high tendency to be boyfriend and girlfriend at camp then break up when we went home. We told ourselves and our friends at camp that we were just friends.

The truth, however, is that I grasped for more. I wanted the excitement of romance and the comfort of being liked. The next day, I wrote Chelsea a note saying that I couldn't bear to have the end of camp signal the end of our friendship. Even though we lived far apart, could we please keep in touch through the mail? She agreed.

This was Mistake Number Two. Now, letter writing is a fine thing. I wrote to several friends, both guys and girls, after camp. But Chelsea and I did more than keep in touch. For several months, we wrote each other almost every day. The relationship not only cost a small fortune in postage; it bordered on obsession. When I wasn't writing to Chelsea or poring over the letters she had written to me, I was thinking and talking about her.

To any rational person, we were obviously much more than friends. Even though we closed each letter with "Friends forever," these poetic missives dripped with romantic overtones. We scattered "I miss you's" and "I can't stop thinking about you's" heavily throughout each epistle. On one note Chelsea wrote "I love you in Christ" in bright letters at the top of each page.

Just friends? Yeah right.

As I look back, I'm amazed at how I justified my actions. "How can this be wrong?" I reasoned. "We live thousands of miles apart, have never kissed, and can't even date!" What I failed to realize is that you don't have to live next door to someone to pursue intimacy prematurely. And you don't have to go on dates to overstep the limits of friendship; the U.S. Postal Service allows you to accomplish this despite distance.

The relationship didn't end well. Chelsea and I became more

serious. We even flew out to visit each other. But eventually we began to see that we had less in common than we had originally thought. Our romantic ardor had glossed over our incompatibilities.

When Chelsea met another guy from school and began being "just friends" with him, I became jealous. We couldn't evaluate our "friendship" objectively, we hurt each other's feelings, and eventually our letter writing died along with our relationship—another premature romance ended in heartbreak.

I ended up in the same situation I had been so determined to avoid.

How did it happen? When did our friendship develop into something more? Could I ever be just friends with a girl, or was it entirely impossible?

Brothers and Sisters

Though I've sometimes failed in my attempts to walk the fine line between friendship and romance with girls, I do believe that guys and girls can have life-enriching, non-romantic friendships. In fact, it's important that we do.

The apostle Paul instructs his spiritual son Timothy to treat younger women "as sisters, with absolute purity" (1 Timothy 5:2). God wants us to be committed to absolutely pure and vibrant relationships. Paul is reminding us that we're family. Through Christ we've been adopted by God. "The relationship between Christian brothers and sisters is not something we create," writes Elisabeth Elliott. "It's already established. We are members of one another. We are related." In these already established relationships, we need to strive for both total purity and true friendship.

At another point Paul tells Timothy what the *focus* and *purpose* of these relationships should be. "Flee the evil desires of youth," he writes, "and pursue righteousness, faith, love and peace, along with those who call on the Lord out of a pure heart" (2 Timothy 2:22).

Paul is telling Timothy to find brothers and sisters in Christ who will call on the Lord alongside him. For Paul, Christian friendship has

God's glory as its goal. It's not aimless or merely for the sake of a good time. Paul's primary concern is not that we develop social skills—he wants our friendships to be an expression of a passionate desire for God and His glory.

The point here is that we need each other to do this. We need the perspective, the encouragement, the "sharpening" that comes from friendships with members of the opposite sex.

What do brother-sister relationships look like? They're characterized by biblical fellowship, affection, and genuine care. Let's look at each one more closely.

BIBLICAL FELLOWSHIP

Brothers and sisters in Christ refuse to be satisfied with superficial relationships. They're not content with the kind of shallow and meaningless conversations that typify TV sitcoms—their passion isn't to appear witty, but to grow in godliness. They want to share in the most important aspect of their lives—the reality of Jesus Christ and His work in them. *This* is what biblical fellowship is all about. It's discussing and sharing what God is teaching us and *doing in us*.

I know a group of single men and women who congregate at a local restaurant every Sunday after church to discuss the pastor's sermon. They talk openly about what God convicted them about. They drink large volumes of iced tea. They pray for each other. Through these meetings they've developed deep friendships.

AFFECTION

I'm the oldest of seven kids in my family. I have five brothers and one sister. I love all my brothers, but little Sarah has a special place in my heart. There's an affection for her that's unique. My brothers understand and feel the same way about her. We want to protect her and care for her. She's our sister, and that means something very precious.

This is what Paul was getting at when he instructed Timothy to treat the younger women as sisters. Ladies, the reverse is true for you: God wants you to view the younger men as brothers. Totally separate from romantic interest and dating, we're to care deeply about each other. In another place Paul describes more of what this looks like: "Love each other with genuine affection, and take delight in honoring each other" (Romans 12:10, NLT).

Do you have this kind of godly affection for brothers and sisters? Do you pray for them? Do you look for ways to encourage them in their walk with God? Do you delight in honoring them? One of the small groups in my church comprised of single men and women has done a great job of fostering this kind of environment. On one occasion the men in the group planned a special dinner for the ladies, served all the food, and even had special gifts for each girl. After the meal the men shared reasons why they respected and valued the friendship of each girl. This is genuine affection!

It's important to be consistent—don't show kindness only to those people you have a romantic interest in. Instead show kindness to all your brothers and sisters. This isn't flirting for the purpose of stirring romantic interest in someone; it's showing Christlike brotherly love.

GENUINE CARE

Brothers and sisters look out for each other. They comfort each other. They find ways to serve each other. And at times they have to gently challenge and rebuke each other in love. It's all part of genuine care.

My friend Christina was beginning to develop a very close relationship with a non-Christian guy. Though she brought him to church several times and told me and others that she was "reaching out" to him, I was concerned about the nature of their relationship. I called her one day and asked if she was being drawn into a romantic relationship with someone who didn't follow Christ. She admitted that she was and had already made some foolish decisions about where and when they were alone. God used our conversation to convict Christina and reveal the dangerous path she was on. She involved her mom and other girlfriends and changed the nature of her friendship with the guy.

I've benefited from being challenged as well. My friend Heather provided this kind of care for me when she talked to me about the way I was interacting with the girls in our singles group. She pointed out ways I had focused a lot on certain girls and things I said and did that could cause girls to think I was interested in them romantically. It was hard to hear, but God used Heather's words to help me change.

SIDE BY SIDE

Gentlemen, are you the kind of friend to the girls in your life that you will one day hear from their husbands, "Thank you for being a brother to my wife"? Ladies, do you relate to your guy friends in a way that would make their future wives want to seek you out and thank you for being a sister to their husbands?

When we're single, we can become obsessed with the questions of how we're going to get to know our future husband or wife. "How do we have the friendships *we need* in order to one day get married?"

It's not wrong to ask these questions, but I think we need to see that an even more important question is, "How can I start being the kind of friend to the opposite sex that they *need?*" We need to take our focus off of ourselves and look for ways to serve those around us.

God wants us to neither run from each other nor use each other in an indulgent pursuit of short-term romance. He's calling us to be firmly committed to biblical friendships. In brother-sister relationships, men and women spur each other on to godliness—they stand against wickedness together, they seek God together, they honor one another and grow in grace side by side.

The Abuse of a Harmless Thing

Though we should take advantage of the benefits of guy-girl friendships, we must not forget their boundaries. If we want to enjoy anything good, we must recognize its limitations, and friendship with the opposite sex is no exception. No matter how beneficial or innocent something may be, when we ask too much of it, we can cause harm to ourselves and to others. Solomon passed down this principle using the analogy of food: "If you find honey, eat just enough—too much of it, and you will vomit" (Proverbs 25:16). Just because something is good doesn't mean we should gorge on it. Like healthy eating, healthy friendships require self-control and moderation.

Let's look at four important steps involved in maintaining healthy friendships with the opposite sex.

1. UNDERSTAND THE DIFFERENCE BETWEEN FRIENDSHIP AND INTIMACY.

We can more clearly see the elusive line between friendship and "more than friendship" when we understand the difference between friendship and intimacy.

Friendship is about something other than the two people in the relationship; intimacy is about each other. In a true friendship, something outside the two friends brings them together. C. S. Lewis writes, "We picture lovers face to face, but friends side by side; their eyes look ahead." The key to friendship is a common goal or object on which both companions focus. It can be an athletic pursuit, a hobby, faith, or music, but it's something *outside* of them. As soon as the two people involved focus on *the relationship,* it has moved beyond friendship.

Can you see how this progression took place in my story with Chelsea? In the beginning, we based our friendship on the fact that we were both at a leadership camp for two weeks. We shared other common interests, such as tennis and the piano. Our interaction based on these things remained within the bounds of friendship.

But we had little reason to continue our friendship from a distance. We couldn't participate in common interests side by side over the miles. We had no basis for continuing the relationship at such an intense level except for the fact that we were interested in each other. If we had truly pursued friendship, we would have seen that our friendship couldn't transcend the limits of geography and lifestyle. We'd have admitted that the only thing bringing us together was common attraction.

But we didn't. Thus the focus of our correspondence moved from our common interests to our relationship. We turned from walking side by side to being face to face, focused on one another.

The reason most guy-girl friendships cross into romance is that the people involved don't understand the difference between friendship and intimacy. Too often we confuse the two. With Chelsea, I said I wanted friendship, but I really wanted intimacy. I wanted someone to care about me and love me. My actions betrayed my true desire for the excitement and comfort romance provides.

Were these desires wrong? No, but they were ill-timed. I'm not saying that we should avoid intimacy. We shouldn't. Intimacy is a great thing. But it's the reward of commitment. If we're not ready or capable of committing ourselves to someone, we aren't ready to pursue intimacy.

Remember the analogy we used in chapter 2? Pursuing intimacy without commitment is like going mountain climbing with a partner who, once halfway up the mountain face, isn't sure he or she wants to hold the rope. The last thing you want to hear thousands of feet in the air is that your partner feels tied down in your relationship.

This is exactly what I selfishly did to Chelsea. I wanted the thrill of romance, but I wasn't really ready to make a commitment. Does this mean that I should have married Chelsea because I started the relationship? No, it means I shouldn't have started an intimate relationship with her in the first place.

Understanding the difference between friendship and intimacy can help us stay within the bounds of friendship until we're ready for the responsibility of an intimate relationship.

2. BE INCLUSIVE, NOT EXCLUSIVE.

The second step in being just friends with the opposite sex is to include others in activities instead of isolating ourselves with just one person. We can avoid this by going out of our way to involve friends and family in our lives.

Please note that including others doesn't mean finding a token chaperone so you can go on a date. I know more than one couple who brings along a younger brother or sister when they go out so they can call their date a group activity. The local Bible college that many of my friends attend has a rule that students can go out only with a "social unit" of three people. I once had friends invite me to do something with them only to find they had invited me because they needed an extra person to complete a social unit. Thanks, guys! Neither of these examples had the needs of the third party in mind. For all intents and purposes, the younger sibling or the third piece of the social unit might as well be bound and gagged in the trunk!

I'm not talking about inclusion for the sake of appearances. Instead, inclusion must stem from a sincere desire to involve as many people as possible. We should start with a final goal in mind—such as fellowship, service, prayer, or study of God's Word—then seek to involve others.

When we find ourselves balking at including others, we need to ask ourselves whether friendship is the real motive of our relationship.

3. MAKE A PRIORITY OF SAME-SEX FRIENDSHIPS.

We need to make sure our friendships aren't *only* with members of the opposite sex. Let's not forget the importance of strong friendships with members of the same sex.

I've made the mistake of neglecting same-sex friendships many times in my life. Without meaning to, I'd stop investing in my relationships with other guys. In group settings, I'd gravitate to the girls. It was fun—girls were more interesting, and besides, they were "just friends." But it wasn't right. I was neglecting my brothers and being lazy by doing what was easy and enjoyable for me.

Maybe you're a girl and you've done the same thing. You find it more enjoyable to be with the guys and find little need for close girl-friends. One woman told me why she thought some females find friendships with males easier. "When your friends are guys, they give you attention that girls don't offer," she said. "And because girls know how other girls think—how we can play games—it's sometimes easier to be friends with guys. You can get away with not being as real."

Although this isn't always the case and many guy-girl friendships are "real," she makes an important point. A lack of same-sex relationships shouldn't be written off as merely a personality preference.

There is a chance we're being lazy or selfish by avoiding relationships that would cause us to grow in character.

By not developing and maintaining same-sex friendships we're also being short-sighted. After marriage it won't be appropriate (or appreciated by our spouse) to have lots of close friends of the opposite sex. The necessity of same-sex friendships will be even more obvious. They'll be an important source of encouragement, counsel, perspective, and accountability.

Building strong friendships with other men in my church has helped me to grow in my love for God. We meet several times a month both for fun and for serious discussion. They know the areas in my life where I struggle with sin. They keep me accountable. They pray for me and encourage me in my faith. I do the same for them. Their friendship provides something that no girl—not even a wife—could. The same is true for women. Your friendships with other women will provide a unique form of encouragement and support that guy friends just can't offer.

4. SEEK OPPORTUNITIES TO SERVE, NOT TO BE ENTERTAINED.

The late Kurt Cobain captured the attitude of today's culture with the line, "Here we are; now entertain us." I believe that, unfortunately, many Christians have made Cobain's lyric the refrain of their friendships.

In my opinion, our cultural obsession with entertainment is really just an expression of selfishness. The focus of entertainment is not to produce something useful for the benefit of others but to consume something for the pleasure of self. And a friendship based on this self-serving, pleasure-seeking mindset can easily slip into a similarly self-serving romantic relationship that meets the needs of the moment.

But when we shift our relationship orientation from entertainment to service, our friendships move from a focus on ourselves to a focus on the people we can serve. And here's the incredible thing: In service we find true friendship. In service we can know our friends in a deeper way than ever before.

Stop a moment and give this idea some thought. What can you learn about someone by sitting next to him or her in a movie theater? In contrast, what can you learn about someone while serving side by side with that person? When we break out of that mindset and begin to serve others, we not only please God, but we also receive the blessing of one of the most fulfilling experiences of friendship—two people (or more!), side by side, traveling toward a common, noble purpose.

I'm not saying we can't ever seek entertainment. But I do think we should seek to serve first. So serve soup with a friend at a mission before you sit at home and watch a video. Get a group of friends together to teach the fifth-graders at church before you ask the youth pastor to take you to the water-slide park. Start a band, like my brother, that leads worship at church and other Christian events before you go to a concert or buy another CD. Produce before you consume; serve before you seek entertainment.

No Accident

Being just friends with members of the opposite sex doesn't happen by accident. We have to work for and guard our friendships. Like magnets, men and women are designed to attract each other. But until we're ready to be "stuck for life," we need to avoid premature intimacy. How do we do that? By respecting the limitations of guy-girl friendships and relating to others within the framework given by God's Word. In Romans 12:10–11 we read, "Be devoted to one another in brotherly love. Honor one another above yourselves. Never be lacking in zeal, but keep your spiritual fervor, serving the Lord."

What's our relationship to each other? We're brothers and sisters in Christ.

How do we treat each other? With honor.

And what's the secret to our zeal? Service—side by side for God's glory.

Guided by this attitude, being "just friends" can be just plain awesome.

CHAPTER ELEVEN

Guard Your Heart

How to Fight the Pollutants of Lust, Infatuation, and Self-Pity

E MILY SPRAWLED LAZILY on the bed as she watched Jessica pack. "I bet I know what'll happen when you get to school," she said suddenly.

"Oh, really," Jessica replied distractedly. She was more concerned now with how to organize the mess of clothing, shoes, and makeup that covered her bedroom floor.

"Yeah, really," Emily said as she threw a pair of socks at Jessica. She could tell when she wasn't being taken seriously.

"You're going to get there, meet some guy, and fall in love. Then you'll have to crawl back—on your knees—and beg me to forgive you for all the hassle you've given me about dating. Oh, I can't wait until you have a boyfriend!"

If anyone besides Emily had said this, Jessica would have been angry. But coming from her best friend—infuriating though she was—Jessica had to smile.

"Emily, I've told you before that it's not a matter of not wanting to fall in love," Jessica said as she crammed another pair of jeans into her suitcase. "I'm just not interested in playing games and chasing after pointless relationships…like *some* people I know."

Choosing to ignore Jessica's jab, Emily replied, "You just wait; college will change your mind."

When the Rules Don't Fit the Game

Seven months later, Jessica sat in her room looking out the window at a squirrel hopping across the parking lot. It was one of those rare moments in the afternoon when the dorm was quiet enough for Jessica to think. "Maybe Emily was right," Jessica mused as she replayed the conversation in her mind. College had turned her world topsy-turvy. All of her idealistic views of love and the perfect courtship seemed out-of-date and old-fashioned. She'd arrived at college so sure of things; now she didn't know what she believed.

Growing up in a small town with few Christian guys, Jessica hadn't really considered dating. Her girlfriends provided her plenty of companionship; and homework, volleyball, and softball kept her busy.

During her junior year of high school, Jessica heard a speaker at a youth conference give a message called "A Biblical Perspective on Romance." He talked about how dating often contradicted scriptural principles. Jessica was surprised at how much sense the speaker's ideas made. She had never consciously "not dated," but now she understood why she had always felt uncomfortable with the concept. Jessica began mentally cataloging the many times her friends had been hurt by dating relationships that had turned sour. Hadn't she seen how negative dating could be?

Thus Jessica began her search for the "right" way of doing things. Or, as Emily put it, Jessica went "ballistic on her anti-dating campaign." She scoured the Bible for insight, read books, listened to tapes on the subject, and spent more than a few evenings talking—often arguing—with her friends about the merits and pitfalls of dating.

From this quest Jessica emerged with her own "rules of romance," like a modern-day Moses descending from Mount Sinai with the Ten Commandments. She felt sure that her list of dos and don'ts would solve the world's relational problems…or at least keep *her* from experiencing them. First, Jessica wouldn't allow herself to get bogged down in short-term relationships. Until she felt she could pursue marriage, dating was out; she would go out with guys only in groups.

At the point when romance was appropriate, a guy who showed interest in her would first have to talk with her parents. From this point, Jessica had every detail of the courtship process planned like a carefully written screenplay. After checking out the prospective suitor, Mom and Dad would give the young man permission to woo her, the two of them would fall hopelessly in love, and the sun would shine at their outdoor wedding.

All this was good. Wisely, Jessica had developed high standards. In fact, her rules were sound. But her method of developing her guidelines lacked something. Yes, her rules made sense, but they were just rules—they hadn't come to life in her heart. And only those beliefs that spring from the heart can ever hope to stand firm against the rushing winds of emotion.

When Jessica arrived at college (a very conservative Christian school chosen in part because of its strict guidelines), she found to her dismay that all the outward rules she had counted on did nothing to control the feelings that suddenly began to well up inside her. She had never interacted with so many handsome, godly guys on a daily basis. Jessica had never had a problem turning down a date with the non-Christian guys back home. But when tall, clean-cut Eric gazed at her with his penetrating brown eyes as he discussed that morning's chapel sermon, Jessica felt her resolve melting.

To make matters worse, she couldn't look ten feet without seeing a couple. They were everywhere! Three out of her four roommates had boyfriends and looked on her lack of attachment in bewilderment, if not disdain.

Inside, Jessica began to covet her roommates' relationships. Suddenly the thought of having a boyfriend seemed so comforting.

She found herself daydreaming about certain guys. *What if so-and-so is "the one"? What did he really mean when he said such-and-such? Does he like me?* With all these thoughts swimming in her head, Jessica became wistful and discontented. No matter what she did, she'd think, *If only I could share this with someone.* She had more than enough girlfriends and several guy friends, but they hardly fulfilled the longing she felt.

To make things even more difficult, guys were beginning to ask her out. Were any of them husband material? Not quite, but one was cute…. Deep down, Jessica knew she was doing all the things she had resolved not to, but did it even matter now? Her standards and rules seemed worthless.

Getting Acquainted

The human heart doesn't like taking orders from the mind. The time will come for all of us when we won't *feel* like doing the godly, responsible thing we've resolved to do. The question is, how will we respond when our hearts lead a full-scale rebellion? If we don't prepare ourselves for an uprising, we'll feel tempted to abandon our principles and standards.

"As I grew into womanhood," writes Elisabeth Elliot in *Passion and Purity,* "and began to learn what was in my heart, I saw very clearly that, of all things difficult to rule, none were more so than my will and affections." The sooner we get acquainted with the contents of our hearts, the better. Too many of us are blissfully unaware of how deceitful the core of our beings can truly be. When we think "heart," we picture cutesy, red, cutout valentines. But often, if we'd really examine our hearts, we'd find lies, selfishness, lust, envy, and pride. And that's the abridged list! It's like discovering your sweet old grandmother's picture on the FBI's Most Wanted list at the post office.

But though we might be surprised by the contents of our hearts, God is not. He understands how easily it can be swayed in the wrong direction.

The Deceitful Heart

The Bible is replete with warnings about the nature of the human heart and instructions to make our top priority watching over it. Proverbs 4:23 tells us, "Above all else, guard your heart." How should we do this?

First, picture guarding your heart as if your heart were a criminal tied in a chair who would like to break free and knock you over the head. In other words, protect yourself from your heart's sinfulness. Keep a wary eye on your heart, knowing that it can do you damage if it is not carefully watched.

"The heart is deceitful above all things..." we read in Jeremiah 17:9. "Who can understand it?" Though the advice of many well-meaning people today is to "follow your heart," the Bible warns that your heart can lead you in wrong, even deadly, directions. Our hearts lie. Something can "feel" right and be completely wrong.

Julie, a nineteen-year old who worked as a receptionist in a doctor's office, found herself deeply attracted to her boss, a married man who was beginning to make advances toward her. She wanted to act on her attraction and play along with his flirting. Her heart told her to give in to her feelings. Should she have listened?

Fortunately, Julie's convictions resisted the whisperings of her heart. She quit her job and confessed her temptation to a Christian friend, who prayed with her and promised to keep her accountable.

Julie wisely guarded her heart by thinking through the consequences of her actions. If she followed her feelings, she would sin against God, carry the memory of the affair into her future marriage, and possibly ruin the man's marriage and family. Recognizing these things exposed the ugliness of Julie's heart's desires. Getting away from the temptation and finding an accountability partner were further precautions to ensure that she didn't fall prey to her own sinful heart.

Do you face a potentially precarious situation that your heart wants you to pursue? Like Julie, do whatever it takes to guard your heart and keep it in submission to God.

Maintaining a Pure Spring

Next, picture guarding your heart as if it were a fresh spring of water that you want to drink from daily. The Bible tells us the heart is "the wellspring of life" (Proverbs 4:23), the source of our attitudes, words, and deeds. If we fail to keep our hearts clean, the rest of our lives will stagnate and become dirty.

Peter Marshall, the former chaplain of the United States Senate, loved to tell a story called "The Keeper of the Spring." This simple tale beautifully illustrates the importance of constantly maintaining the purity of our hearts.

An elderly, quiet forest dweller once lived high above an Austrian village along the eastern slopes of the Alps. Many years ago, the town council had hired this old gentleman as Keeper of the Spring to maintain the purity of the pools of water in the mountain crevices. The overflow from these pools ran down the mountainside and fed the lovely spring that flowed through the town. With faithful, silent regularity, the Keeper of the Spring patrolled the hills, removed the leaves and branches from the pools, and wiped away the silt that would otherwise choke and contaminate the fresh flow of water.

By and by, the village became a popular attraction for vacationers. Graceful swans floated along the crystal-clear spring, the mill wheels of various businesses located near the water turned day and night, farmlands were naturally irrigated, and the view from restaurants sparkled.

Years passed. One evening the town council met for its semiannual meeting. As the council members reviewed the budget, one man's eye caught the salary paid the obscure Keeper of the Spring. "Who is this old man?" he asked indignantly. "Why do we keep paying him year after year? No one ever sees him. For all we know, this man does us no good. He isn't necessary any longer!" By a unanimous vote, the council dispensed with the old man's services.

For several weeks nothing changed. But by early autumn, the trees began to shed their leaves. Small branches snapped off and fell into the pools, hindering the rushing flow of sparkling water. One afternoon, someone noticed a slight yellowish-brown tint to the water in the spring. A few days later, the water had darkened even more. Within a week, a slimy film covered sections of the water along the banks, and a foul odor emanated from the spring. The mill wheels moved slowly; some finally ground to a halt. Businesses that were located near the water closed. The swans migrated to fresher waters far away, and tourists no longer visited the town. Eventually, the clammy fingers of disease and sickness reached deeply into the village.

The shortsighted town council had enjoyed the beauty of the spring but underestimated the importance of guarding its source. We can make the same mistake in our lives. Like the Keeper of the Spring who maintained the purity of the water, you and I are the Keepers of Our Hearts. We need to consistently evaluate the purity of our hearts in prayer, asking God to reveal the little things that contaminate us. As God reveals our wrong attitudes, longings, and desires, we must remove them from our hearts.

Pollutants

What are some things God will ask us to remove from our hearts, especially concerning our dating mentality? "Do not love the world," John warns us, "or anything in the world.... For everything in the world—the cravings of sinful man, the lust of his eyes and the boasting of what he has and does—comes not from the Father but from the world" (1 John 2:15–16). In this passage, John gives us three catgories of worldly things that pollute our hearts: sinful cravings, lust, and prideful comparison with others. Can we apply these items to romantic relationships? I think so. In fact, most of our struggles in relationships seem to involve desiring what we shouldn't desire, lusting after what God has forbidden, or complaining about what we don't have. These "pollutants" specifically manifest themselves in relationships as infatuation, lust, and self-pity. Let's examine all three more closely.

INFATUATION

You've probably experienced it—the constant thoughts about some-one who has caught your eye, the heart palpitations whenever that person walks by, the hours spent dreaming of a future with that spe-cial someone. It's infatuation, and I know it well, having experienced it myself!

Many of us have a difficult time seeing infatuation as potentially harmful. But we need to examine it carefully, because when you really think about it, infatuation can be a sinful response to attraction. Any time we allow someone to displace God as the focus of our affection, we've moved from innocent appreciation of someone's beauty or per-sonality to the dangerous realm of infatuation. Instead of making God the object of our longing, we wrongly direct these feelings toward another human. We become idolaters, bowing to someone other than God, hoping that this person will meet our needs and bring us fulfill-ment.

God is righteously jealous for our hearts; after all, He created us and redeemed us. He wants us to focus our thoughts, longings, and desires on Him. He lovingly blesses us with human relationships, but He first calls us to find our heart's delight in Him.

In addition to diverting our attention from God, infatuation can cause problems for us because it is most often founded on illusion. When infatuated with someone, we tend to build up that person in our imaginations as the perfect guy or girl. We think we'd be happy forever if that person would return our affections. Of course, we can only sustain our silly crush because we've substituted fantasy for all the information we lack about the person. As soon as we get to know that person's true identity and discover that our "perfect" man or woman is human like everyone else, our dreams fade and we move on to a new crush.

To break out of this pattern of infatuation, we must reject the notion that a human relationship can ever completely fulfill us. When we find our hearts slipping into the fantasy world of infatuation, we should pray, "Lord, help me to appreciate this person without elevating him (or her) above You in my heart. Help me to remember that no human can ever take Your place in my life. You are my strength, my hope, my joy, and my ultimate reward. Bring me back to reality, God; 'give me an undivided heart'" (Psalm 86:11).

My dad likes to say that when you let God be God you can let humans be human. When we place God in His rightful place in our lives, we don't struggle so much when human relationships let us down. In direct contrast, when we make another human our idol, God can't be our God.

After placing God first in our lives, we need to continue to avoid infatuation by resolving *not* to feed attraction. "Don't nurse a crush!" a girl from Brooklyn, New York, told me when I asked her how she beats infatuation. And she's right. Attraction only grows into infatuation when we pamper it.

Each time we find ourselves attracted to someone, we have a choice to either leave it at attraction or allow our imaginations to carry us away. I was once a guest on a radio talk show and afterward talked to the producer, a single woman in her thirties. She told me teenagers aren't the only ones who deal with crushes. This beautiful, intelligent woman still had to resist infatuation as an adult. She made a statement that I have found very helpful. "Joshua," she said after telling me about how a gentleman had recently been pursuing her, "I want to stay focused on God. Until the right man comes along, I refuse to feed romantic expectations and let my heart get carried away."

For her, feeding romantic expectations meant daydreaming about a guy on the way home from work, putting his picture on the refrigerator, and giggling about him with friends. At the right time in a relationship, each of these activities might be appropriate, but before the proper time, she knew these actions would only lead to fantasy-based infatuation.

How about you? Have you found yourself succumbing to infatuation, removing your focus from God, and fantasizing about the "perfect" partner? Perhaps you need to take a step back and evaluate the role infatuation plays in your life.

LUST

The second poison that often threatens the purity of our hearts is lust. To lust is to crave something sexually that God has forbidden. For example, when as a single man I look on a woman who is not my wife (which right now means every woman) and immorally fantasize about her, I am lusting; I am setting my heart on something God has placed off-limits. Sexual desire within marriage is a natural and appropriate expression of sexuality; after all, God gave us our sex drives. But God also gives us specific commands forbidding us to indulge in those desires before we marry.

To fight lust in our lives, we have to detest it with the same intensity God does. Unfortunately, we often do not. An experience I had while visiting Denver, Colorado, opened my eyes to my own laxity toward lust. One afternoon I was walking from my hotel to the convention center downtown. A group of three guys walked past me in the opposite direction. They smiled in a way that seemed odd. They whispered and laughed as they passed me, and for some reason, those actions made me uncomfortable. What was bothering me? I pushed my discomfort out of my mind and went on. But a few moments later a car pulled up alongside me. The same three guys were inside. This time, I could in no way mistake their intent or the reason I'd felt strange—these guys were homosexuals and were checking me out. They whistled, winked, and laughed at my bafflement. Finally they sped away, leaving me to fume.

I'll never forget the anger and disgust I felt at that moment. I was outraged to have served as the object of their lust, to have their eyes crawling over me. It was so wrong, so filthy.

I remember turning to God in self-righteous anger and hissing through my clenched teeth, "Those people are so sick!"

The gentle rebuke God whispered to my heart caught me off guard.

"Joshua, your smug heterosexual lust is just as misplaced, just as disgusting in My sight."

This realization floored me. My contempt at the lust of those three men was *nothing* in comparison to the disgust God feels at the lust in *my* heart, even though society condones and expects it. God states that when I look at a woman lustfully, whether she is on the street, on a billboard, or in a movie, I'm actually committing adultery with her in my heart (Matthew 5:28). That's serious!

How many times have I felt lust for a passing girl in the same way as those homosexual men felt for me? How many times have my eyes slid across a woman's body like a "slug on a rose," as Cyrano de Bergerac so aptly described it? Am I as repulsed by lust in *my* life as I am by lust in others? Beilby Porteus writes, "What we are afraid to do before men, we should be afraid to think before God."

We should seek to completely remove lust from our minds. We should pray, "Create in me a pure heart, O God" (Psalm 51:10). Help me to be like Job, who made a covenant with his eyes not to look lustfully at others (Job 31:1). Forgive me for pampering lust in my life; help me to guard against it faithfully. May the "meditation of my heart be pleasing in your sight, O LORD" (Psalm 19:14).

Finally, we need to avoid those things that encourage wrong desire. For one girl I know, guarding her heart against lust meant throwing away all her secular romance novels. She felt convicted that the constant sensuality those books featured was totally inappropriate for her to read, making her heart rich soil for seeds of lust. Another friend attending college stopped spending his afternoons at the beach because the bikini-clad girls there were too great a temptation for his eyes. Another male friend decided to abstain from all movies for six months. All three of these are examples of people, each with different weaknesses, who are guarding their hearts from those things—books, locations, movies—that lead to sinful desires.

When we evaluate our lives honestly enough to recognize our own lust and see the sorrow it causes God, we'll want to destroy lust…before it destroys us.

SELF-PITY

The final pollutant of our hearts is self-pity. In a sense, self-pity is the worship of our circumstances. When we indulge in feeling sorry for ourselves, we turn our focus from God—His goodness, His justice,

His ability to save in any circumstance. And as we turn away from God, we cut ourselves off from our only source of hope.

We can so easily allow self-pity to seep into our hearts. When we feel lonely or crave someone to love and be loved by, it seems we have every reason in the world to complain, to sulk angrily because we've received a bum deal.

But do we really have reason to complain when we consider the Cross? As I try to follow God's plan for relationships and as a result forego short-term dating, I'm sometimes tempted to fall into a "martyr" mentality. "Oh, woe is me! Here I am, suffering for righteousness!" What foolishness! In my more objective moments, I imagine God's response to my self-pity as similar to the message of a popular T-shirt: "Would you like some cheese with your whine?" Spending my time sighing over what I've given up doesn't impress God; obeying Him with joy does.

Self-pity is a sinful response to feelings of loneliness. We don't sin when we feel lonely or admit a desire for companionship, but we do sin when we use these feelings as an excuse to turn from God and exalt our own needs.

Do you often find yourself focusing on your own sorry state and not relying on God to do His best for you? If so, then you probably need to take an honest look at your tendency toward self-pity. If you need to, you can defuse self-pity by doing several things. First, stop basing your happiness on how you compare with other people. Don't get sucked into the comparison game. Too many people waste their lives pursuing things they don't really want just because they can't bear the idea of someone having something they don't. Ask yourself this question: "Am I really lacking something in my life, or am I just coveting what someone else has?"

Next, when you feel those old feelings of self-pity rising, redirect them into compassion for others. Look around for someone who might share your feelings of loneliness, and find a way to comfort that person. Get your focus off your needs, and help meet someone else's.

Finally, learn to use feelings of loneliness as an opportunity to draw closer to God. A girl in her midtwenties who recently married told me that she saw loneliness as God's call to her heart. "When I felt lonely, I would think, *God is calling me back to Him,*" she told me. During these times she learned to pour out her heart to God and talk with Him. Now she wouldn't trade those intimate moments with God for the world.

He Knows All Things

The job of guarding our hearts is a big responsibility. It takes place in the secret places of devotion. In honest prayer and meditation on God's Word, we scrape the film of infatuation, lust, and self-pity from our hearts. And as with the Keeper of the Spring, the work is never done. We must police our hearts with "faithful, silent regularity."

Yes, our hearts are deceitful, but the promise of 1 John 3:20 gives us hope in our labor: "For God is greater than our hearts, and he knows everything." God's strength can help see us through the upheavals of our emotions. And we can take comfort in the knowledge that He doesn't view our plight from a distance, shaking His head at our weakness. Jesus, the Son of God who Hebrews 7:25 tells us "always lives to intercede" for us, has endured the same feelings of loneliness you and I have, and He understands how it feels to face temptation. He will help and sustain us as we trust in Him and faithfully guard our hearts.

CHAPTER TWELVE

Redeeming the Time

Making the Most of Your Singleness

LOOK AT THIS," my mom said, handing me a card. "We're invited to a reception for Jenny and her new husband."

I stared at the invitation and the couple pictured on it. My jaw dropped. "I can't believe this," I said. "Jenny Renquist is married? This is impossible!"

"What do you mean, it's impossible?" Mom asked.

"I liked her in eighth grade!" I said. "How can she be married?"

"She met a nice guy, and they got married. It happens all the time."

"Why is it happening to all the girls I used to like?" I whined.

"You haven't talked to or thought about Jenny for years," my mother reprimanded. "Don't get wistful all of a sudden."

"I'm not," I said, looking at the picture again. "Mom..."

"Yes?"

"I think my biological clock is ticking."

"Boys don't have biological clocks."

"They don't?"

"No."

"Oh."

Marriage on the Brain

Whether or not you have a biological clock, and whether or not it's ticking, marriage will inevitably sneak up on you. Your friends' wedding invitations will begin arriving by the dozens. Suddenly, what once seemed far off and unimaginable has become very real. At this point in your life, people who find out you're unattached often get that matchmaking gleam in their eyes. If you've reached this stage, then you know what I mean. All of those around you mentally pair you up with every available member of the opposite sex they know.

Being single and "of marriageable age" is a precarious state. Even if marriage isn't at the forefront of your mind, it's guaranteed to be on the minds of those around you. My family proved this to me when I turned twenty-one. In my family, we have a tradition of writing letters to each other on our birthdays. The letters I received on my twenty-first birthday really caught me off guard. Why? Because of the consistent references to the "special someone" who evidently, in the opinion of my parents and younger brother, would pop up any day.

My mom started the trend with this sentence: "I know it will be hard to let you go when you meet that one we're all waiting and praying for."

The one they're all waiting and praying for? I thought. *Good grief, Mom!* I brushed off her comment as a lapse into IWGS (I Want Grandchildren syndrome).

Amused, I put down my mom's letter and started reading my dad's. His was full of fatherly advice, but the closing lines picked up the marital theme: "Finally, expect to meet her someday soon, if you haven't met her already. She will be prepared for you by God because 'a good wife is from the Lord.' When you know you have found her, be patient—you needn't rush. But neither should you need to delay things. Marry her within the year and count on God to help you take care of her."

I swallowed hard when I read those words. I put down the letter, then picked it up and read the lines again. "Expect to meet her soon"?

Wow! My dad had never discussed marriage in such serious terms. It seemed so heavy, so grown-up.

Then I opened the letter from my twelve-year-old brother and roommate, Joel. He had designed it on the computer and printed it out on my dad's color printer. *Surely,* I thought, *Joel couldn't have indulged in this marriage silliness.* I was wrong. The end of his note read, "I really treasure sharing a room with you, knowing that some-day soon you'll be sharing a room with someone else."

I burst out laughing. My mom was waiting and praying, my dad was expecting me to meet her soon, and my brother was already dis-cussing the wedding night! Nobody had mentioned marriage when I turned eighteen, nineteen, or twenty. But now it was the talk of the town! If I hadn't known better, I might have thought my family had met in a back room and plotted to get me out of the way by marrying me off as quickly as possible.

What Do I Do Now?

Although my family didn't want to push me into matrimony prema-turely, their letters did remind me that I had entered a new season of life. At this point in my life, marriage is no longer impossible. If God brought the right person into my life I could, theoretically, do some-thing about it.

This realization is exhilarating, but it's also a little confusing. God *hasn't* brought the right person into my life. My friends who have met and want to marry Mr. or Miss Right may face obstacles such as get-ting their finances lined up and figuring out housing, but at least they know what they have to do. They've mapped out a course. But my path isn't so clear.

If you've reached the same stage, maybe you're asking the same questions I'm asking: Does the fact that I could get married mean I should make it a priority to find someone? Do I assume I'll get married soon or act as if I never will? What am I supposed to do *now?*

Hustle While You Wait

Fortunately, we have a source to turn to when these questions arise. I've found some guidance in the book of Ephesians. Paul writes, "Be very careful, then, how you live—not as unwise but as wise, making the most of every opportunity, because the days are evil" (Ephesians 5:15–16). Another version reads, "See then that you walk circumspectly, not as fools but as wise, redeeming the time" (NKJV).

My mom uses the phrase "hustle while you wait" to express the same idea. If one of us children stands around, picking at food while she cooks dinner, Mom will snap, like a football coach to his players, "Don't just stand there! Hustle while you wait!" That means set the table, put away groceries, or load the dishwasher; be productive during a lull in the action.

My mom has an intolerance for wasted time. I think God has the same intolerance. He has entrusted us with gifts and talents, and He expects us to guard and use them wisely. Will we give Him a return on His investment in us? Even though we don't know the next step regarding our romantic relationships, we still have work to do. We have bad habits to get rid of, good habits to develop, and character to build. Let's hustle!

Yes, we'll still have a lot of questions—we may not know whom or when we'll marry. But we must not allow what we *can't know* to hinder us from acting on what we *do know*. And what do we know? We know that we have today to move with resolute energy toward maturity and Christlikeness, a calling of every Christian whether he or she will marry next week or ten years from now.

When we focus on "redeeming the time," we'll not only make the most of each moment; we'll also prepare ourselves for the next season of our lives. Our faithfulness in small things today earns us the right to handle bigger responsibilities down the road.

Watering Camels

In the Old Testament, Rebekah is a young woman who "redeemed the time" by faithfully fulfilling her current obligations. We could learn a few things by revisiting the story of how she prepared for, met, and married her husband. The story begins when Abraham sends his oldest and most trusted servant to his hometown to find a wife for his son Isaac. Catherine Vos continues the story this way:

At last, after several days of travel, he reached the place where Abraham's brother Nahor now lived. This city was called Haran. Outside the city was a well of water. In that dry country there was often only one well for a whole city. Every night the young girls of the city went out to the well, with tall pitchers balanced on their heads. They let down their pitchers into the well and drew water. Then they carried it home on their heads for the family to use.

When Abraham's servant came to Haran, he made his camels kneel down by the well. It was evening—just the time when the young girls always gathered around the well to draw water.

Abraham's servant believed in God. He had come safely on his journey and had reached the city to which Abraham had sent him. But he thought to himself, "How shall I be able to tell which young girl is the one God wants Isaac to have for his wife?" He kneeled down on the ground beside the well and bowed his head. He prayed, "O LORD God of my master Abraham, help me this day! When the daughters of the people of the city come down to draw water, and I say to one of them, 'Let down your pitcher, I pray you, that I may drink,' and she shall say, 'Drink, and I will give your camels drink also,' let that be the one whom Thou hast appointed as a wife for Isaac."

God often answers prayer almost before we have asked, and He did so this time. Before the servant had finished praying, a very beautiful girl named Rebekah came to the well. The servant thought, "Can this be the right one?" He ran to her and said, "Let me, I pray you, drink a little water out of your pitcher."

The girl said very politely, "Drink, my lord, and I will draw water for your camels also, till they have finished drinking." She took the pitcher down from her head and let him drink. Then she emptied the rest of the water into the drinking trough for the camels. She kept drawing water till all the camels had had a drink.

The servant was very much astonished to have her say and do just as he had prayed that she might. Had his prayer been answered so soon? When the camels had had enough water, he gave Rebekah a rich, gold ring which he had brought with him, and he put on her arms two beautiful gold bracelets.

Then he asked her, "Whose daughter are you? Is there room in your father's house for us to stay?"

She answered, "I am Nahor's granddaughter. We have plenty of room for you to stay with us, and straw and food for your camels." Nahor was Abraham's brother. When the servant heard this, he was so happy that he bowed his head down to the ground and worshiped, saying, "Blessed be the LORD God of my master Abraham, who has led me to the house of my master's family."

The rest of the story (which you can read in Genesis 24) tells how Rebekah agreed within two days to return with Abraham's servant to marry Isaac, a man she had never met. The tale is, without question, an amazing example of God's sovereignty over every detail of our lives. In their own day, these events were astonishing; today, separated by thousands of years and very different cultures, we find them even more astounding. And yet, as with all of God's Word, we can learn a lesson from this story that transcends time and culture.

Although we don't study the story as a model of how every

couple should meet and marry, we can learn from Rebekah's attitude and actions. In an article entitled "The Adventure of Current Obligations," Gregg Harris points out an important principle of the story: "Rebekah was able to meet God's divine appointment for her life because she was faithfully carrying out her current obligations."

For Rebekah, the trip to the well that particular evening was nothing special. She made that trip every night. And she'd probably watered more than a few camels. Yet though her task was mundane, she had a quickness to her step and a ready willingness to serve others. These qualities put her in the right place at the right time with the right attitude when God intended to match her with Isaac.

We all have our own camels to water—current relationships and responsibilities we can too easily take for granted. If we're wise, we'll see our duties not as unimportant ways to bide our time, but as springboards, launching us into God's plan and purpose for our future.

Practice Now

For a moment, take stock of your current attitude. Are you so caught up in dreaming about marriage that you're neglecting your present responsibilities as a son, daughter, brother, sister, or friend? Or are you redeeming the time, fulfilling those responsibilities God has given you today?

We cannot ignore our current responsibilities and expect to magically gain the strength of character and virtue that will make us good husbands and wives. If we aren't faithful and growing in the relationships we have now, we won't be prepared to pursue faithfulness and growth in marriage later.

Someday I want to be a godly husband. I want to nurture my wife, love her, respect her, and protect her. How can I train for that? I believe that God has given me a mother and sister in order to practice understanding and honoring women. If I can't love and serve my mother and sister today, what makes me think I'll be ready to love and serve a wife in the future? I have to practice now. The reverse is true for girls and their dads and brothers. Girls can view their relationships with the men in their lives as training sessions for loving and respecting a future husband.

Marriage won't transform us into new people; it will only act as a mirror, showing what we already are. We have to practice now what we want to be in the future. Let's look at a few areas we can prepare for while we're still single.

PRACTICE INTIMACY

While we want to avoid premature intimacy in romantic relationships, we should practice intimacy in other committed relationships, starting with our families. God has given us families so that we can learn the art of sharing life.

A close female friend of mine realized she had developed bad communication habits with her parents. Whenever they tried to talk to her, she would clam up and refuse to share her feelings. "It finally hit me," she told me. "If I shut out the people closest to me now, I'll do the same thing someday to my husband." To reverse this trend, my friend now works hard to build intimacy and openness with her folks. Instead of retreating to her bedroom after dinner, she hangs around and talks with them. Instead of shutting them out of her life, she invites them in. This process, which wasn't easy at first, is teaching her skills she'll need one day as a wife.

PRACTICE SEEKING GOD WITH OTHERS

A newlywed friend told me that before he got married, he was used to having uninterrupted time in the morning to pray and write in his journal. Now he had to make room for prayer and devotions with his wife as well as both of their private times with God. "I never knew how confusing it could be to coordinate two spiritual lives!" he said.

Each of us must develop a dynamic, growing, personal relationship with God. This involves practicing the spiritual disciplines of prayer, meditation, Bible study, Bible teaching, and involvement in a local church. But in preparation for marriage, we also need to learn to seek God with another person. Again, we don't want to practice this discipline with a romantic interest until we're ready to pursue committed intimacy. But we can develop this habit with other important people in our lives. You might start this process with your family then branch out to pray and study the Bible with safe, nonromantic friends from church. Learn to share with others the lessons God teaches you. Learn to pray with someone else. Be honest about your areas of weakness, and ask God for a trusted person to keep you accountable in those areas.

Recently I was with a group of four friends—one guy and three girls. We had spent the day hiking then returned to my house to relax and talk. One of the girls began to talk about how God had dealt with her on different issues of obedience. Her testimony led to a spontaneous time of prayer as we joined hands, worshiped God, and lifted up each other's needs to the Lord. It wasn't a forced, unnatural show of "talking about God" so we'd look spiritual; we were merely discussing the most real aspect of our lives—Jesus. What an awesome example of redeemed time! We not only built each other up, but we also learned how to seek God side by side. And that transparency and ability to discuss spiritual issues will one day sustain our future marriages.

PRACTICE FINANCIAL RESPONSIBILITY

We need to learn not only how to make money and support ourselves, but also to manage our money responsibly. Now is the time to learn how to budget, save, and tithe consistently.

For several weeks, my parents met with me and two other friends to help us each create personal budgets. One of our assignments was to record every penny we spent for a week. What a revealing exercise! I was completely unaware of how much money I wasted eating out. Although I still go out, I've now put a limit on how much I can spend on food in a month. Another guy I know found he was investing an inordinate amount of his paycheck from his job at the Gap right back into the company! He cut back his clothing budget and began saving and giving more.

Because singles don't have as many responsibilities as married folks, we can quickly develop poor habits of spending. We need to make sure we don't develop patterns with money that will jeopardize a marriage or, even more important, waste God's resources.

In addition to learning about budgeting, balancing a checkbook, and car and health insurance, we also need to establish our own philosophy toward finances. What kind of lifestyle does God want us to pursue? What is His view of money and possessions? Left unanswered, these issues can cause serious stress in a marriage and serious regret if we waste our lives pursuing the wrong things.

A book that has helped me tremendously in this area is *Money, Possessions and Eternity* by Randy Alcorn (Wheaton, Ill.: Tyndale, 1989). Also, Larry Burkett has written excellent books and study guides about practical issues related to finance; many are designed specifically for young adults.

PRACTICE PARENTHOOD

Children are not one of the risks of marriage; they are one of the rewards. And the work of becoming a good father or mother starts when we're single. Right now we can take notes from the veterans and practice those parenting qualities we'll one day want as we raise our future children.

God has blessed me with five younger siblings ranging from age two to thirteen. While being a parent is in a totally different league from being a brother, I can "practice" parenthood now by investing time in my siblings' lives, by doing my best to direct them toward godliness, and by including them in my activities. I've changed my share of dirty diapers; I've fed, washed, and clothed my brothers and sisters. In doing so, I've learned a little of the responsibility and joy that accompany parenting.

Look for opportunities to practice and learn now, whether or not you have younger siblings. I'm inspired by Jeanne, a friend of my family's, who takes this preparation seriously. As the youngest in her family, she never had the opportunity to be around small children. To make up for lost time, Jeanne volunteers free of charge as a mother's helper for a family with seven kids. One day a week she goes to this family's home and apprentices in all the household activities, including watching the children, cooking, doing laundry, and cleaning.

Another important part of preparing for parenthood is observing good parents in action. If your own parents can't provide this, find parents in your church to follow as examples. One friend told me he tries to observe and spend time with dads he wants to be like. He asks himself these questions: "How do these godly dads teach their kids to love God? How do they handle discipline? How do they teach and instruct their kids?" Though he doesn't get any college credit for it, I have a feeling his study will pay off when he one day faces the biggest test of manhood: being a dad himself.

PRACTICE PRACTICAL LIFE SKILLS

What are practical life skills? Just ask your parents to let you take over the maintenance of your house, including shopping, planning menus, and cooking meals for a couple of months—you'll soon find out.

Although these sorts of skills aren't glamorous, they are an important part of managing a household. We have no excuse for not preparing ourselves in this area. And the best preparation is actually doing it. A few years ago, my mom had me start doing all the grocery shopping for the family. I also had to cook one dinner each week. At first, I didn't always cook the most appetizing meals for my family, but I got better!

Though I've improved my skills in the kitchen, I'm still woefully unprepared in the area of home maintenance. I'm sure you have your own weak spots, too. Let's get to work strengthening them! If you don't know where to start, sit down with your folks or a godly man or woman in your church, and ask them to outline the skills they find necessary to run a household. Write down these skills, and establish a plan to master each one.

Marriage Is Not the Finish Line!

Perhaps I've struck a chord with you. Maybe you can think of a few ways to redeem your time so you can feel confident that you're using your singleness for God's glory. What might you put into practice even today?

We can actively choose ways to prepare ourselves for marriage if God wills it for our future. But let's remember the real reasons for our preparation. Learning the skills that would make us a good spouse is a by-product of growing in maturity and Christlikeness. But though marriage is optional, developing Christlike qualities is not. Each of us must develop love, humility, patience, forgiveness, and responsibility in our own lives.

As singles, part of good stewardship involves gaining the skills we'll need in marriage. But marriage is not the finish line. Statistically speaking, most of us will eventually marry. But we need to make sure we "redeem the time" to glorify God, not to earn brownie points from Him so that we can demand marriage. We prepare and develop our characters so we can become as flexible and useful for Him as possible, no matter what He plans for our future. Biological clocks can tick all they want—let's redeem today!

PART FOUR

Looking Ahead

CHAPTER THIRTEEN

Ready for the Sack but Not for the Sacrifice

How to Have a Biblical and Realistic Vision of Marriage

FOR A YEAR IN high school, I operated a small production company that videotaped weddings. This job was, to say the least, an interesting way to make a living.

An engaged man and woman would contract with me to videotape their wedding so they could remember every last detail of their special day. When that day came, I would arrive at the church several hours early with my camera, lights, tripod, and sound-mixing gear in tow. I then spent the entire day recording, or you might say intruding on, every memorable moment. I captured on tape the ladies fussing over the bride's veil; through the lens I watched the nervous conversation between the groom and his best man. During the ceremony, I recorded the special music, the candle lighting, and the exchanging of vows. At just the right moment, I zoomed in for the kiss.

At the reception, I immortalized images of guests stuffing their faces with appetizers, punch, and those minty candies popular at weddings. Of course, I couldn't miss the cake cutting, the bouquet and garter tosses, or the final event when, amid a shower of birdseed, the couple piled into a waiting car and sped away. (One couple even had me go to the airport to film them boarding a plane for Hawaii…she was still wearing her wedding gown and he, his tuxedo!)

But my real work came *after* the wedding. While the lovebirds enjoyed their honeymoon, I spent my days staring at a monitor, editing many hours' worth of footage down to a seamless, slick sixty-minute tape. I cut the bloopers and blunders so everything looked perfect.

If you watched one of those videos without knowing all the fast-forwarding and splicing I had done, you could mistakenly believe that the wedding had gone off without a hitch. You wouldn't know that the bride's mother and sister argued fiercely over where to pin the veil or that the tuxedos barely arrived in time or that a nephew stuck his hand in the punch bowl. In an edited video, everything flows naturally, the bride and groom look like stars in their own movie, and the soft background music gives all of it the feel of a fairy tale.

It's beautiful and romantic, but it's not reality.

An Edited Vision of Marriage

Unfortunately, many young adults have a view of marriage as limited and unreal as the wedding videos I used to create. These people think of married life as one grand, thrilling moment after another—the everyday, mundane parts of marriage are safely edited from the picture.

A friend once told me that the girls in her dormitory spent hours poring over bridal magazines. They'd choose their gowns and bridesmaid dresses. They'd endlessly compare engagement rings. While there's nothing wrong with their anticipation, my friend wondered if these girls devoted too much energy and attention to what is, in reality, a very small part of marriage. "Marriage is much more than a wedding ceremony," write Gary and Betsy Ricucci in their book *Love that Lasts*. "A wedding is an event, but a marriage is a state of being. It's not a one-time act; it's a lifelong commitment to be developed and maintained." One can only hope that those girls will give thought to what comes *after* the wedding festivities. Will they be prepared for the development and maintenance that marriage will demand?

Girls aren't the only ones guilty of reducing marriage to a single aspect. We guys have our own immature view of marriage, too. I'm ashamed to admit that I struggle with the tendency to equate marriage with sex. When I picture being married, I almost immediately picture going to bed with my wife, as if that's all married people do! Yes, husbands and wives do have sex, and there's nothing wrong with looking forward to that important part of married life, but that can't be the extent of my vision. If I foster the idea that sex is the chief purpose and end of marriage, I'll one day enter marriage unprepared, and I'll face certain disappointment. I may be ready for the sack, but am I ready for the sacrifice of married life?

How about you? Do you find yourself concentrating on one aspect of marriage to the exclusion of all others? Or can you maintain the big picture and prepare yourself for all that marriage will be?

Duly Considering

As singles we face the important task of cultivating a balanced, biblical understanding of God's purpose and plan for marriage. Marriage is not to be, in the words of an old wedding sermon, "enterprised lightly or wantonly to satisfy man's carnal lusts and appetites, but reverently, discreetly, advisedly, soberly and in the fear of God, duly considering the causes for which matrimony was ordained."

How should we view marriage? According to this sermon, reverently, discreetly, advisedly, and soberly. These words, rich in meaning, give us a vivid and vast picture of marriage. *Reverence* means "a profound respect mingled with awe." *Discretion* means "discernment or good judgment." To do something *advisedly* means "to carefully consider" it. And to approach something *soberly* means "to be well-balanced, unaffected by passion, excitement, or prejudice."

Do these qualities define our approach to marriage? All too often, the answer is *no*. I've heard people validate the union of two people solely because, in their opinion, the two would have beautiful babies. That may be true, and there's nothing wrong if they do, but if we place importance on such an issue, we obviously don't view marriage very highly. We need to leave behind the giddy idea that marriage is a game or some sort of "prom for grown-ups," in which being a cute couple matters most.

Instead, we need to sober ourselves up with a cold splash of reality. We need to understand God's purpose for marriage as well as our responsibility in marriage. Fortunately, God's Word gives us both in clear terms. The Ricuccis write in *Love that Lasts,* "You don't have to read very far in the Bible to be astounded by God's perspective on this most sacred and significant relationship." Gary and Betsy go on to outline this perspective in their book. They've given me permission to excerpt (and slightly adapt for singles) the section in which they answer the question, "What is marriage?"

> *Marriage is the first institution* (Genesis 2:22–24). It was ordained before the family, before civil government—even before the church.

> *Marriage depicts the supernatural union between Jesus and the church* (Ephesians 5:31–32). One of the most beautiful analogies God uses to define His relationship with us is that of a marriage. To grasp this is both inspirational and sobering. People should be able to look at our marriages and say, "So that's what the church is like? That's what it means to have a relationship with Jesus?"

> God intends to cultivate the same abundant, unconditional love between a husband and wife as He Himself has for us. Marriage is a profound and marvelous mystery established by God for His glory.

> *Marriage is the event God has selected to consummate all of time* (Revelation 19:7). God has had at least two thousand years to make preparations for honoring His Son at the end of the

age. It's significant that God has not scheduled the corona-
tion of the Lamb or the graduation of the Lamb. Instead He
has ordained the marriage supper of the Lamb. Why marriage? Because it speaks of union and intimacy as nothing
else does. The greatest thing God could plan for Jesus was to
present Him with His radiant Bride. No wonder we are so
deeply moved when a bride walks down the aisle. Marriage
is a holy and wonderful gift. And one day we will be called
to account for our stewardship of this gift.

Marriage is to be held in honor (Hebrews 13:4). The Amplified
Version of the Bible elaborates on this verse, noting that marriage should be esteemed worthy, precious, of great price,
and especially dear. This requires that we guard against any
thought that dishonors or belittles marriage.

When I (Gary) stop at the grocery store for milk and
bread, I will often buy flowers for Betsy. On one particular
trip, when I reached the cashier, he joked, "What's the matter—you in the doghouse?" It would have been easy to
laugh along with him and join in the joke. But I wanted him
to know my marriage was important to me. Here was a
chance to challenge his misconception, to sow in his mind a
seed of hope about the tremendous potential of marriage. So
without getting self-righteous about it, I answered, "No—I
just love my wife."

Your future spouse is created in the image of God. Your marriage
will be a sacred relationship.

The Ricuccis also say that we should use "every opportunity to
defend the sanctity of marriage." Even though the Ricuccis' book tar-
gets married couples, I think singles can defend the sanctity of
marriage as well.

How can we do this? Earlier, I told you about my friend whose
dorm mates' view of marriage went little further than a discussion of
engagement rings and wedding gowns. How could my friend have

defended the sanctity of marriage in that setting? Without dampening the other girls' enthusiasm for their future weddings (they have every right to be excited about the big day), she could have helped them by gently reminding them of other important aspects of married life. She could have asked questions such as "How are you going to raise your kids? How are you going to keep the communication lines open with your husband?" These kinds of questions can encourage proper perspective and balance in our view of marriage.

In my case, the next time a group of my male friends begins to discuss marriage as merely the opportunity to have sex, I can, once I've adjusted my own attitude, challenge their limited and immature view. Even though I'm single, I can help myself and others to have a high view of marriage by rejecting attitudes and words that belittle or reduce it from the place of honor God has given it.

How can *you* encourage others to hold marriage in high esteem?

The Crucible of Marriage

The Ricuccis' final point needs our extra attention:

Marriage is a refining process. Conflict will occur in every marriage. When issues erupt between the two of you, it will be easy for one to blame the other. "If you would just leave the air conditioner on when it gets this hot, I wouldn't get upset!" The fact is, your spouse won't make you sin. They simply reveal what's already in your heart. One of the best wedding gifts God will give you is a full-length mirror called your spouse. If He were to attach a card it would say, "Here's to helping you discover what you're really like. Congratulations!"

From a distance, singles see the glow of married life and think only of how it will warm them. And in many ways it will. But we forget that God wants to use the fire of marriage not only to comfort us, but also to refine and cleanse us from our selfishness and sin. We come to warm our hands by the fire of marriage; God wants to throw us into it!

I don't want to give (or believe!) the idea that marriage will be all pain and discomfort. But marriage won't be unending bliss and personal fulfillment either, and if we don't realize this, our experience of marriage will be extremely uncomfortable. As quickly as possible, we must dispel any selfish notions that marriage is about what we can get instead of what we can give.

The Fine Print of Dreams

Advice columnist Ann Landers once gave some helpful advice regarding the work marriage involves. One of her readers lamented the unrealistic ideas many girls had of marriage, beseeching, "Why don't you level with them, Ann?" Landers replied:

> I have leveled with the girls—from Anchorage to Amarillo.
>> I tell them that all marriages are happy.
>> It's the living together afterward that's tough.
>> I tell them that a good marriage is not a gift,
>> It's an achievement.
>> That marriage is not for kids. It takes guts and maturity.
>> It separates the men from the boys and the women from the girls.
>> I tell them that marriage is tested daily by the ability to compromise.
>> Its survival can depend on being smart enough to know what's worth fighting about.
>> Or making an issue of or even mentioning.
>> Marriage is giving—and more important, it's forgiving.
>> And it is almost always the wife who must do these things.
>> Then, as if that were not enough, she must be willing to forget what she forgave.
>> Often that is the hardest part.
>> Oh, I have leveled all right.
>> If they don't get my message, Buster,

It's because they don't want to get it.

Rose-colored glasses are never made in bifocals

Because nobody wants to read the small print in dreams.

In our daydreams about marriage, we too often forget what a drastic course of action marriage really is. We read the captivating headlines but neglect to read the exacting fine print. What does the fine print say? That good marriages require work, patience, self-discipline, sacrifice, and submission. That successful marriages take "guts and maturity" and, we should add, a biblical understanding of God's purpose and plan for it. Only when we cultivate these qualities and disciplines can we carry out our responsibilities and experience true joy and fulfillment in marriage.

Man Enough to Answer

I want to close this chapter with a challenge to young men. While Ann Landers's advice to girls calls them to awaken from childish dreams and realize that marriage takes work, the following poem by Lena Lathrop, entitled "A Woman's Question," speaks particularly to men. It chills me every time I read it. Lathrop's words show me to be the immature boy that I am, stopping me in my tracks and daring me to be man enough to treat a woman right. Some of the poem's wording might seem old-fashioned, but the message is timeless.

Do you know you have asked for the costliest thing
Ever made by the Hand above?
A woman's heart, and a woman's life—
And a woman's wonderful love.

Do you know you have asked for this priceless thing
As a child might ask for a toy?
Demanding what others have died to win,
With the reckless dash of a boy.

You have written my lesson of duty out,
Manlike, you have questioned me.
Now stand at the bars of my woman's soul
Until I shall question thee.
You require your mutton shall always be hot,
Your socks and your shirt be whole;
I require your heart be true as God's stars
And as pure as His heaven your soul.

You require a cook for your mutton and beef,
I require a far greater thing;
A seamstress you're wanting for socks and shirts—
I look for a man and a king.

A king for the beautiful realm called Home,
And a man that his Maker, God,
Shall look upon as He did on the first
And say: "It is very good."

I am fair and young, but the rose may fade
From this soft young cheek one day;
Will you love me then 'mid the falling leaves,
As you did 'mong the blossoms of May?

Is your heart an ocean so strong and true,
I may launch my all on its tide?
A loving woman finds heaven or hell
On the day she is made a bride.

I require all things that are grand and true,
All things that a man should be;
If you give this all, I would stake my life
To be all you demand of me.

If you cannot be this, a laundress and cook
You can hire and little to pay;
But a woman's heart and a woman's life
Are not to be won that way.

To girls reading this book, I pray this poem serves as a reminder to keep your standards high. Require all things that are "grand and true." As you consider the possibility of marriage, don't lower your standards for a moment; any guy who asks you to do so isn't worth your time.

And to the guys, we have our work cut out for us, don't we? My hope for us is that we would truly grasp the costliness, the priceless-ness, of a woman's love. It is no small thing, no game, to invite a girl to accompany us through life. May we earn the right to make such a request by striving to be men of integrity—men whose hearts are oceans "strong and true." Then, and only then, should we stand at the bars of a woman's soul and ask to gain entrance.

CHAPTER FOURTEEN

$\backsim$

What Matters at Fifty?

Character Qualities and Attitudes That
Matter Most in a Life Partner

As I PONDER THE foreverness of marriage, one question keeps rattling through my mind: "What qualities should I look for in a wife?" Perhaps you wonder the same thing as you consider spending the rest of your life with one special person. What would make someone the perfect mate for you?

When I think of that question, I know the answer entails many deep, internal characteristics, but in everyday life, I still find it difficult to get past the superficial. A cute girl walks in the room, and all my common sense evaporates. How many times have I made a complete fool of myself by falling head over heels for someone simply because of her charm and beauty? Too many times.

To cure this tendency, I've created a little game. When I meet a beautiful girl and I'm tempted to be overly impressed by her external features, I try to imagine what this girl will look like when she is fifty years old. (If this girl is with her mother, this game doesn't take too much imagination.) This girl may be young and pretty now, but what happens when the beauty fades? Does anything within her beckon to me? Is it her character that radiates and draws me toward her, or is it just the fact that her summer dress shows off a little too much of her tan? So what if her feminine outline captures my eye today? When pregnancies add stretch marks and the years add extra pounds, will something in this girl's soul continue to attract me?

Things That Last

As we consider what's important in a marriage partner, we need to get past the surface issues of looks, dress, and performance in front of others. "The LORD does not look at the things man looks at," God says. "Man looks at the outward appearance, but the LORD looks at the heart" (1 Samuel 16:7). Proverbs 31:30 tells us, "Charm is deceptive, and beauty is fleeting." The same verse tells us that the kind of person who deserves praise is the one who "fears the LORD."

We're too easily impressed by image; God wants us to value qualities that will last. Wisely choosing a marriage partner requires that we get back to the essentials of a person's character and attitude.

In this chapter we'll look at the character qualities and attitudes important in a spouse. But as we do so, we also want to ask, "Am I cultivating these in my own life?" Let's be careful to maintain a humble attitude of self-examination. We need to concentrate not only on *finding* the right person but, more important, on *becoming* the right person.

Character

"Character is what you are in the dark when no one but God is watching," writes Randy Alcorn. "Anyone can look good in front of an audience, or even in front of their friends," he continues. "It's an entirely different thing to stand naked before God, to be known as you truly are on the inside." We don't define a person's true character by the image that person wishes to convey or the reputation he or she hides behind, but by the choices and decisions that person has made and makes each day.

It takes real wisdom to observe a person's character. It also takes time. William Davis writes, "Your reputation is learned in an hour; your character does not come to light for a year."

Glimpses of True Character

How do we evaluate a person's character? How do we get past image and reputation to catch a glimpse of who a person really is?

As we evaluate someone's character (including our own), we need to carefully observe three areas—how the individual relates to God, the way he or she treats others, and the way this person disciplines his or her personal life. These areas are like windows into a person's character. "As the daylight can be seen through very small holes, so little things will illustrate a person's character," writes Samuel Smiles. "Indeed, character consists in little acts, well and honorably performed."

Let's look at some of the "little acts" that can tell us more about a person.

HOW A PERSON RELATES TO GOD

A person's relationship to God is the defining relationship in his or her life—when this relationship is out of order, every other relationship will suffer. Scripture plainly states that a Christian should not even consider a non-Christian for a spouse. "Don't team up with those who are unbelievers," the Bible says (2 Corinthians 6:14, NLT). Both you and the person you marry must have a dynamic, growing, personal relationship with Jesus Christ. The question is not merely "Are you and a potential spouse saved?" but rather "Are both of you in love with Jesus Christ? Will you place Him before even each other?"

"This is one of those beautiful paradoxes of biblical truth," write David Powlison and John Yenchko. "If you love and want your spouse more than anything, you will end up selfish, fearful, bitter, or disillusioned. If you love Jesus more than anything else, you will really love and enjoy your spouse. You will be someone worth marrying!"

Once, in a conversation about relationships, two Christian girls told me that they find focus on God one of the most attractive qualities in a guy. "It's obvious when he really loves the Lord," my friend Sarah said. "When he's telling you about his love for God, you can tell that he's not distracted by you."

"Exactly!" affirmed Jayme. "It's funny because the guys that really go out of their way to impress girls don't impress me at all. They make me nauseated."

Look for, and work on becoming, a man or woman who, as a single, seeks God wholeheartedly, putting Him before anything else. Don't worry about impressing the opposite sex. Instead, strive to please and glorify God. Along the way you'll catch the attention of people with the same priorities.

How a Person Relates to Others

The second window to a person's character is his or her relationships with others. Watch how a potential partner (and you) relate to the following people:

Authorities. How does a potential mate respond to people in authority? Does this person respect the authority of a boss or pastor even if he or she disagrees with that authority figure? A guy who can't follow legitimate orders will have difficulty holding a job or receiving pastoral correction when needed. A girl who can't respect a teacher's or coach's authority will have difficulty honoring her husband. Look for, and strive to become, a person who respects God-given authority.

Parents. You've probably heard this sage advice before: "The way a guy treats his mom is the way he'll treat his wife." It's true. The same goes for the way a girl relates to her dad. I'm not saying that a person who has had a bad relationship with his or her dad or mom can't have a good marriage. By God's grace we can overcome old patterns. But we do need to ask, "If he can't be loving and gentle with his mom, why should I believe he'll be loving and gentle with me as his wife?" or "If she can't respect her dad, will she be able to respect me as her husband?"

Don't forget to evaluate your own life. How do you relate to your parents? Can you improve the way you interact with them so you'll know how to honor your future spouse? If you'd *really* like the answer to these questions, ask your parents to tell you their perspectives on your relationship with them.

The opposite sex. There's a huge difference between genuine friendliness and flirtatiousness. Learn to distinguish between the two. No one wants to marry a flirt. Guys, if a girl flits like a butterfly from one guy to the next, always in need of male attention, do you really think marriage will suddenly change her? Girls, do you want to marry a man with a wandering eye? And what about yourself? Where do you stand on the friendly-flirtatious scale? Do you need to change your attitudes and actions toward members of the opposite sex?

Companions. A person's companions are the people who influence and shape him or her. In this category, the *way* someone treats his or her friends is not as important as *who* these friends are. A. W. Tozer observed, "There is a law of moral attraction that draws every man to the society most like himself. Where we go when we are free to go where we will is a near-infallible index of character."

Who are a potential marriage partner's closest friends? How do these friends act? What do they value? If they're caught up in partying and living recklessly, the person who spends time with them will probably share those pursuits. What about your companions? Are you pursuing relationships with people who encourage you in your walk with the Lord? Or do your friends drag you down? Don't underestimate how much your close friends shape your character.

PERSONAL DISCIPLINE

The third window to character is how a person disciplines and conducts his or her personal life. "Habit," writes Charlotte Mason, "is the greater part of nature." The things we do involuntarily, almost without thinking, reveal our character.

When we consider this category, we need to note the difference between sinful habits and simply annoying habits or poor manners. Everyone has habits that another person will find silly or irritating.

My dad drives my mother crazy with the way he eats corn on the cob. His method is reminiscent of an old typewriter: *Munch, munch, munch, munch, kaching! Munch, munch, munch* down the next row. This may not be the best table manners, but it isn't a sinful habit. Instead of concerning ourselves with issues such as these, we need to examine whether a potential spouse (or we ourselves) fosters habits that are disobedient to God or that reveal a deeper disregard for others.

The following are a few areas in which a person's habits give us a glimpse into his or her character. Watch these closely in your own life, too.

How a person uses time. I heard Elisabeth Elliot give a speech in which she said that one of the things that first attracted her to Jim Elliot was the fact that he memorized Scripture as he waited in the cafeteria line. That observation told her that Jim was disciplined and efficient.

The way a person spends his or her leisure time tells us what he or she values. Does this person fill free time with mindless hours in front of the TV? Does this person cultivate his or her mind and build relationships, or does he or she run to the next distraction? Seek to find someone (and to be the kind of person) who uses time wisely.

How he or she handles money. The way a person handles money is one, if not the surest, indicator of character. At his nineteenth birthday party, my friend Andy asked people to bring money. But he didn't want the money for himself. Instead, he gave all of it to a Christian outreach effort in the inner city. Andy's attitude toward material things proved him a man of compassion, love, and generosity. It showed that he valued the eternal more than the material.

Is the person you're observing (or are you) caught up in clothing, cars, and other material things? Does this person think through purchases, or does he or she spend impulsively, prone to splurging? A person's spending habits reveal his or her level of responsibility.

How he or she takes care of his or her body. We should not fault a person because of things he or she cannot control—height, features, and in some cases, weight. Neither should we be overly concerned with the external. However, the way a person cares for his or her body tells us something about that person's character.

First, how does this person dress? A girl who dresses immodestly may catch guys' attention, but what does her clothing say about her heart? A guy who spends his money on the latest style of clothing may have the appearance of "togetherness," but his infatuation with fashion could mean he's too preoccupied with what people think of him (and that he may make poor decisions with his money).

Next, how does this person care for his or her body? Does he or she have disciplined eating habits? Does he or she have a reasonable and consistent program of staying fit? God wants us to maintain the health and condition of our bodies so that we can more effectively serve Him. This does not mean, however, that we should become obsessed with exercise. A person who is too concerned about weight lifting is just as out of balance as the person who doesn't exercise at all.

How would *you* stand up to evaluation in this category? Is there room for improvement in your life?

The Impact of Attitude

After character, attitude is the second essential criteria in choosing a spouse. Attitude is a person's vantage point, the way he or she looks at and reacts to life. For the Christian, this involves more than mere positive thinking. A godly attitude involves God-centered, Bible-based thinking—working to view ourselves, others, and our circumstances from God's perspective.

The following are a few key ways that godly attitudes are expressed:

An Attitude of Willing Obedience to God

As you seek a mate, look for someone who will listen to and act without hesitation on what God is telling him or her. You want someone with an attitude like David's, saying to God, "I will hurry, without lingering, to obey your commands" (Psalm 119:60, NLT). An attitude of willing obedience recognizes the lordship of Jesus in every area of life.

Is the person you're interested in consistently looking for ways to submit more of his or her life to God? Does he or she work to overcome bad habits? Is this person being conformed to today's culture, or does he or she push against it, seeking to be transformed into Christ's image?

Are you working to develop an obedient attitude in your own life? You'll never be perfect or find a perfect mate—we're all sinners—but only people with an attitude of willing obedience to God's Word will continue to grow in godliness and maturity throughout their lives.

An Attitude of Humility

An attitude of humility considers others' needs first. The Bible states, "Do nothing out of selfish ambition or vain conceit, but in humility consider others better than yourselves" (Philippians 2:3). Does the person you're interested in place the needs of others before his or her own? Watch the small things. When he's on the basketball court, how does he act? Even in competition does he seek to serve others? How does she respond when conflict arises in her family? Is she quick to blame the other party or humble enough to share blame and seek resolution? And how do *you* handle these situations?

One of the things I respect most about my dad is his willingness to humble himself before my mom and the rest of my family by confessing sin. If he has spoken a harsh word or acted uncaringly, he doesn't hesitate to seek forgiveness. A lesser man can't do this.

Two people don't keep a marriage strong because they never make mistakes; they keep a marriage strong by maintaining an attitude of humility that is quick to confess sin, put the other first, and seek forgiveness.

An Attitude of Industriousness

Don't judge a person by his or her line of work, but do take note of the attitude with which this person approaches work. An attitude of industriousness is one of willingness to work hard at whatever task presents itself. William Bennett writes: "Work...is not what we do *for* a living but what we do *with* our living.... The opposite of work is not leisure or play or having fun, but idleness—not investing our-selves in anything."

In Proverbs 31:17 the noble wife is described as someone who "sets about her work vigorously; her arms are strong for her tasks." (Of course, industriousness is important for both men and women.) Look for someone who energetically invests his or her life in some-thing important right now. Strive for this attitude in yourself, too.

AN ATTITUDE OF CONTENTMENT AND HOPEFULNESS

An attitude of contentment and hopefulness is one that recognizes God's sovereignty in every situation. It is faith-birthed optimism that looks to God—an attitude more aware of and grateful for the evi-dence of God's grace than of problems needing correction.

Here are a few important questions to ask about the person you're getting to know as well as about yourself: Does this person have complaint or praise on his or her lips? Does he or she nitpick at the faults of others or consistently encourage? Does this person view his or her circumstances with a spirit of hopelessness, or does he or she remain confident of God's faithfulness?

Early in his marriage, the Reverend E. V. Hill and his wife, Jane, faced financial difficulty. He had foolishly invested in a service station, and the business had failed. Money was very tight. Dr. Dobson, who heard Reverend Hill share their story at Jane's funeral, recounts it this way:

> Shortly after the fiasco with the service station, E. V. came home one night and found the house dark. When he opened the door, he saw that Jane had prepared a candle-light dinner for two.
>
> "What meaneth thou this?" he said with characteristic humor.
>
> "Well," said Jane, "we're going to eat by candlelight tonight."

E. V. thought that was a great idea and went into the bathroom to wash his hands. He tried unsuccessfully to turn on the light. Then he felt his way into the bedroom and flipped another switch. Darkness prevailed. The young pastor went back to the dining room and asked Jane why the electricity was off. She began to cry.

"You work so hard, and we're trying," said Jane, "but it's pretty rough. I didn't have quite enough money to pay the light bill. I didn't want you to know about it, so I thought we would just eat by candlelight."

Dr. Hill described his wife's words with intense emotion: "She could have said, 'I've never been in this situation before. I was reared in the home of Dr. Caruthers, and we never had our lights cut off.' She could have broken my spirit; she could have ruined me; she could have demoralized me. But instead she said, 'Somehow or another we'll get these lights on. But let's eat tonight by candlelight.'"

Tears come to my eyes every time I read this story. Mrs. Hill's optimism and readiness to walk through tough times with her husband exemplify the two qualities I desire in my own life and pray for most in a wife. I'm looking for someone who will light candles, not just curse the darkness.

The Cliff

I've shared all these characteristics and attitudes in hopes of clarifying what really matters in a spouse—what to look for in another person and what to work on in our own lives. We should not use these qualities to bash the opposite sex or as an excuse to avoid marriage. No one will achieve perfection in all the areas we've explored. For the man who expects to find a wife who is perfect, Benjamin Tillett had this quip: "God help the man who won't marry until he finds the perfect woman, and God help him still more if he finds her."

We will never find the perfect spouse. If we did, why would he or she want to marry an imperfect person like you or me? Benjamin Franklin said, "Keep your eyes wide open before marriage—half shut afterward." Marriage requires faith in God's provision and a willingness to forgive imperfections—the mercy needed to keep our eyes "half shut" to the flaws.

One young guy e-mailed me about his fear regarding marriage: "How can I possibly get to know a person well enough before marriage to know if she's right? It seems like getting married is like jumping off a cliff." In one sense he's right. Marriage will always be a step of faith. Not a blind leap, but a step just beyond what we can see for certain.

My pastor, C. J. Mahaney, tells the humorous story of how, before his wedding, he reached out his hand to his father-in-law-to-be and said, "Thank you, sir, for trusting me with your daughter." The man replied, "I don't trust you." Then after a long pause he said, "I trust God." This father had his trust in the right place.

We can't trust ourselves, and we can't completely know the person we decide to marry, but we *can* trust God to guide us in our decisions and to help us follow through with our commitments.

True Beauty

While I'm single, I'm working to build godly character in my life and to have the right attitudes. And as I observe the young ladies around me, I'm keeping my eyes wide open. And yes, I'm still playing my little game of asking, "What matters at fifty?" It helps me look past the fleeting issues of youth and beauty and focus on the essentials of character and attitude.

Poor girls, if they had any idea about my game... But then, who knows? Maybe they've been imagining what I'll look like at fifty. Now there's a scary thought!

One of these days, and this is the moment for which I'm hoping and praying, I'm going to meet a girl, and when I imagine her at fifty she'll be even more beautiful than she is today. The years won't detract; they'll only sharpen and mature her. Because with a woman who fears God, whose inner strength draws from the wellspring of His life, time can only add to her true beauty. Of course, the signs of age will emerge, but the spirit that lights up her sparkling eyes will still be young, vibrant, and alive. That's what I want to grow to love.

What will I do when I meet this young woman? I think about that often. I don't know exactly what I'll say. Maybe I'll get down on my knees and beg her to spend the rest of her life growing old with me. We can watch our bodies fall apart and together wait for the day when the Master gives us new ones.

And when I kiss her on our wedding day, I'll revel in the wife of my youth, but I'll whisper in her ear, "I can't wait to see you when you're fifty."

CHAPTER FIFTEEN

Principled Romance

Principles That Can Guide
You from Friendship to Matrimony

WHAT DO YOU DO when you think you've met the person you want to marry? Friendship is great, but how should you proceed from there? How do you get to know that special person better?

Whether you're asking these questions about a specific person or a serious relationship is a ways off, it's helpful to think about the steps between friendship and marriage. Although the main focus of this book is on enjoying singleness and waiting on romance till you're ready for marriage, I hope to give a broad outline of how a God-honoring relationship can unfold.

The Bible doesn't provide a one-size-fits-all program for us. Our lives are too different, our circumstances too unique, and our God too creative to have only one formula for romance. The various ways in which God brings men and women together, like the unique designs of snowflakes, are never quite the same. But just as a one-of-a-kind snowflake can only form at a specific temperature and precipitation, a God-honoring romance can only form when we follow godly patterns and principles.

What Do You Call It?

Many people I meet want a name for these principles. If you're not dating, what are you doing? To be honest, I'm not concerned with what term people assign my convictions. Sometimes when I explain to people how I want a future relationship to unfold they'll say, "That's dating!" or "That's courtship!" What I hope you see is that seeking to obey God and genuinely care for others is far more important than whether we use the word *dating* or *courtship*.

I happen to like the term *courtship*. Sure, it's kind of old-fashioned, but it's full of romance and chivalry. I use it to describe not a set of rules, but that special *season* in a romance when a man and woman are seriously weighing the possibility of marriage. I think it's helpful to distinguish between undefined and directionless romance (what I said goodbye to) and romance that is purposefully headed toward marriage. But the fact that I use the word *courtship* doesn't make me better than people who don't.

None of us should allow a debate over words to distract us from what really matters in relationships. "Dating vs. courtship" isn't the point. I've known "serial courters" who lived like the devil and "saintly daters" guided by integrity and holiness. The terms they used to describe their relationships were meaningless by themselves—the way they lived is what really mattered. Terms don't define us; our lives define our terms.

Today many Christians are disillusioned with the way romantic relationships are handled. We desperately want something better. But the "something better" we long for won't come by putting a new name on old attitudes. *We* have to change! We need *new* attitudes— values that are shaped by Scripture and a radically God-centered view of romance.

In this chapter, I'd like to outline a new pattern for relationships that can help us avoid the problems often encountered in relationships today. The seasons I propose are not a magic formula for a perfect relationship, nor are they the only way for romance to unfold.

But I think they can help us develop godly romantic relationships. These stages are:

1. Casual friendship
2. Deeper friendship
3. Courtship: purposeful intimacy with integrity
4. Engagement

Let's examine these seasons and some principles that can guide us through them.

1. Casual friendship.

When you're just getting to know someone, it's essential that you remember what I call your "relational responsibilities." Let me explain. Imagine you're in a car on a lonely deserted road. No one's in sight, and the smooth pavement stretches out as far as you can see. You know the vehicle can go fast; you just don't know how fast. But you'd like to find out. No one will see you. Why not try it? You throw the car into high gear and roar down the road.

Now imagine you're in the car again, but this time a dear friend sits in the passenger seat. And instead of being on a deserted road, you're in the heart of a busy city, surrounded by other cars and pedestrians. Then out of the corner of your eye, you see a police car. You don't even *think* of speeding. You drive down the street slowly and carefully.

What's the difference between the two scenarios? The difference is that in the first you were an isolated person who only had yourself to worry about. But the second scenario placed you in relationships with others. Instead of being alone, you had responsibilities. If you wrecked the car, you would be responsible for the life of the person strapped in the seat next to you. Your recklessness would also place the lives of the motorists around you in danger. And finally, the policeman's presence reminded you of the traffic laws you should obey. You drove slowly.

The same principle works in romantic relationships. If you start out thinking only of yourself—*Will this person like me? Would he or she make a good husband or wife for me?*—you'll speed into a relationship too quickly and probably run over people along the way. But if you remember that your actions affect others, you'll find the resolve to proceed cautiously and carefully.

Every time you feel attracted to someone, keep in mind that you're involved in three kinds of relationships: your relationship with the person you're interested in; your relationships with the people around you, including family and friends; and most important, your relationship with God. You have a responsibility toward each.

Talking to Myself

I try to remember these three relational responsibilities when I'm first getting to know a girl and possibly find myself interested in her. In the early stages of attraction, I have a difficult time remaining clearheaded. I have to immediately remind myself of my responsibilities. I usually end up having a conversation with myself that goes something like this:

"Josh, what's your relationship to this girl?"

"She's a sister in Christ whom I'm instructed to treat with absolute purity."

"Exactly! She's not just a pretty face or a potential wife!"

"No, she's a child of God. God has a plan for her. He's shaping her and molding her into something special."

"So what is your responsibility to her?"

"My responsibility is to make sure I don't get in the way of what God is doing. I should encourage her to keep her focus and dependence on God."

"Okay, good. Now to whom is your second responsibility?"

"My second responsibility is to the people around me."

"Such as…?"

"Such as the people in the church group, non-Christians who might observe our relationship, and even my little brothers, who watch how I relate to girls."

"Why do you have to care what they think?"

"I have a responsibility to keep the unity of the group here at church; I have a responsibility to model the love of Jesus to outsiders; and I have a responsibility to set an example for other believers."

"And your primary responsibility is to God, correct?"

"Exactly. I am responsible to keep my way pure, serve others as Christ did, and love my neighbors as I love myself."

These kinds of questions can help us gain a proper perspective right from the start and can determine whether a relationship will be God-honoring or merely self-satisfying. Breaking out of the defective patterns in relationships requires that we stop seeing ourselves as the "center of the universe" with other people revolving around our desires. Before we embark on a relationship, we need to sober ourselves by reviewing our relational responsibilities.

2. DEEPER FRIENDSHIP.

Today most people assume that if you get to know someone and you're attracted to him or her, you should dive into a romantic relationship—tell that person you're interested, ask him or her out, go for it! But this isn't necessarily best for the relationship in the long run.

One spring my four-year-old sister was so excited to see the first flowers pushing out of the soil that she plucked a handful of the unopened buds and proudly gave them to my mother. My mother was disappointed by my sister's impatience. "You picked them too soon," she said. "They're a lot prettier when they're allowed to bloom."

We're often guilty of the same impatience in our relationships. Instead of waiting until friendship fully blooms, we rush into romance. Our impatience not only costs us the beauty of friendship as singles; it can also place our future marriages on shaky ground. Strong marriages are built on a solid foundation of the mutual respect, appreciation, and camaraderie of friendship.

When we find ourselves attracted to someone, we need to make building a deeper friendship our first priority. Too often we believe that relating in a romantic, exclusive relationship will automatically mean we'll be closer and know each other better. But this doesn't always happen. Although romance can be a more exciting level of relationship, it can also foster illusion and infatuation, obscuring the true character of each person involved. Remember, as soon as we unleash our emotions in romantic love, our objectivity begins to fade. For this reason, we need to focus on developing a closer friendship with a potential partner before introducing romance.

Friendship-Deepening Activities

The first priority for a guy and girl is to get to know each other better as individuals—to gain an accurate, unbiased view of each other's true nature. How can you do this? First, instead of dropping out of your regular routines to spend time together, look for opportunities to include one another in your real lives. Find activities that pull you both into each other's world of family, friends, and work, as well as areas of service and ministry.

For my friend Jason, a Spanish major, this meant inviting Shelly, a girl he'd become friends with at church to visit the Spanish church he helped translate for one Sunday a month. This activity gave her a glimpse into Jason's love for the Spanish language and the Hispanic people. Another time, Shelly asked Jason to help her teach a Sunday school class for fifth graders. Although they spent the majority of their time in groups during both activities, Jason and Shelly discovered more about each other and deepened their friendship.

Things to Avoid

As your friendship progresses, avoid saying and doing things that express romantic love. The context of a deepening friendship is not the time to talk about your possible future together; it's the time to get to know each other, serve God together in the church, and listen for God's leading. Don't take things into your own hands by flirting or dropping hints about your romantic feelings. And don't encourage your friends to talk about you or to treat you as a couple. When your friends do this, simply invite others to join you in your activities so you can keep from being paired off.

It will take patience and self-control not to express your feelings prematurely, but it's worth it. "I want you to promise…" says the maiden in Song of Songs 8:4 (NLT), "not to awaken love until the time is right." The Wycliffe Bible Commentary says, "Love should not be stirred up before its proper time, because the love relationship, unless carefully guarded, may cause grief instead of the great joy it should bring to the human heart." Proverbs 29:20 states, "Do you see a man who speaks in haste? There is more hope for a fool than for him." Don't play the fool in your relationships by speaking too soon. If you're pursuing a deeper friendship, the other person will already have an idea that you're interested, and you can't avoid this. But expressing these feelings in words often "awakens love" before it's ready.

If you really think about it, the need to blurt out our feelings is usually motivated by selfishness, not by a desire to enhance the other person's life. We want to know if our feelings are reciprocated, and we can't bear not knowing how the other person feels. This kind of selfishness has the potential not only to destroy the delicate beginnings of a relationship, but it can also make us feel like fools later if our feelings change. You'll never regret the decision to wait to express your feelings.

Watch, Wait, and Pray before Moving Past Friendship

One of the most confusing times in a relationship comes when both the guy and the girl question whether or not to move beyond friendship. The right time for deepening the relationship varies among couples, but we can all benefit from patience. It's always wise to take the extra time to get to know the other person better as a friend and to seek God's guidance.

If you feel inclined to deepen a relationship with a special guy or girl, wait on God through prayer. Seek the counsel of a few trusted, older Christians. Ideally, these people should include your parents, a Christian mentor, and other trusted Christian friends. Ask these people to join you in prayer about this person. Invite them to keep you accountable about the relationship and to point out any "blind spots" in yourself and the person in whom you're interested.

Questions to Ask

During this watching and waiting time, both the guy and girl need to ask themselves tough questions such as, "Based on the character I've observed in our friendship, would I consider marrying this person? Am I prepared to move this relationship beyond friendship to pursue marriage?"

Obviously these are very serious questions. Most of the problems we observe in dating relationships result from people taking these questions too lightly. As a result, people date those they would never consider marrying and pursue romantic relationships merely for fun, not because they're ready for commitment. We can avoid the problems resulting from the "dating mentality" only by waiting on God and refusing to pursue romance until we have the go-ahead from four "green lights":

GREEN LIGHT 1: *God's Word*

Based on Scripture, is marriage right for you and the person you're interested in? God established marriage, but He also created boundaries around it. For example, if the person you're thinking about isn't a Christian or has a questionable faith, stop in your tracks. Scripture also warns that some ministries are better carried out by singles; perhaps this truth applies to God's plan for your life. Before proceeding in a relationship, seek God's guidance through His written Word.

GREEN LIGHT 2: *You're Ready for Marriage*

Do you have the balanced, realistic vision of married life that we talked about in chapter 13? Are you aware of and ready for the responsibilities of being a husband or wife? Have you reached a level of spiritual maturity and emotional stability as a single that warrants stepping into a lifelong commitment? Are you ready financially? You need to honestly answer these kinds of questions before proceeding with a relationship.

GREEN LIGHT 3: *The Approval and Support of Your Parents (or Guardians, Christian Mentors, and Godly Christian Friends)*

If you think you're ready for marriage but no one else who knows and loves you agrees, you should probably reconsider. You want the wisdom and viewpoint of those who care about you and can view you objectively. This is not to say that parents or other advisers can never be wrong, but rarely should we proceed without their support and blessing.

GREEN LIGHT 4: *God's Peace*

Finally, you can't replace the peace that comes from walking in God's will. When you pray to God or talk with parents and other Christians, does the idea of marriage feel right, or is it marked by tension and apprehension? Though I'm not suggesting that you base this important decision on your feelings, they can be an added indicator of whether or not you should proceed. Most often you'll feel God's peace only when the previous three green lights are clear.

3. COURTSHIP: PURPOSEFUL INTIMACY WITH INTEGRITY.

Assuming you've gotten all four green lights, you'll face a time when you need to clearly define the purpose and direction of the relationship.

Remember the main problem with relationships today that we discussed in chapter 2? Often our dating relationships lead to intimacy but not necessarily commitment. Many relationships, even serious ones, wander without a clear purpose. They're stuck in the twilight zone between recreational dating and engagement. Neither person knows exactly what the other is thinking. "Are we dating just for fun, or is this serious? What's our commitment?" We want to avoid this state of limbo. Doing so will require honesty and courage on the parts of both people.

The season of courtship is a time to match deepening intimacy with deepening commitment. And this requires that we clearly define that the purpose of the relationship is to consider marriage.

This applies specifically to the guys, who I believe should be the ones to "make the first move." Please don't misunderstand this as a chauvinistic attitude. Men, we're not to lord anything over girls; that's the exact opposite of the Christlike servanthood husbands must show their wives. But the Bible clearly defines the importance of a man's spiritual leadership in marriage (Ephesians 5:23–25), and I believe part of that leadership should begin in this season of the relationship. The girls I talk to, Christian and non-Christians alike, agree. They want the guy to take the lead and provide direction for the relationship.

So how should this happen? I believe that the man needs to say something such as, "We're growing closer in friendship, and I need to be up front about my motives. With your parents' permission, I want to explore the possibility of marriage. I'm not interested in playing the game of being boyfriend and girlfriend. I'm ready to be tested by you, your family, and those who are responsible for you. My desire is to win your heart."

But, you might think, *that's so serious.*

Yes, it is! A woman's heart and future are not things to toy with. That's why the vagueness and squirming on the part of men when it's time to "get serious or get lost" is so reprehensible. There comes a point, gentlemen, when we need to be bold, and I'm sorry to say that too often we lack that boldness. We do girls a great disservice by pursuing romance before we're ready to commit, and then by hesitating when we *should* commit. Enough is enough! Let's grow up.

Girls have a responsibility at this point, too. Women, be extremely honest in your response when a man declares his intentions to you. In some cases, that honesty may demand declining the offer to move beyond friendship. But if you've gotten the same green lights in your life, honesty might mean saying, "I'm ready to test and be tested!" It's a two-way street. The guy works to win your affections, but you're on trial as well. Are you ready to let this special man closer to your heart and be tested by his family?

These are big questions, aren't they? But we need to ask and answer them to escape the limbo of directionless, inappropriately intimate relationships.

Honor Her Parents

In my friend Jason's case, Shelly was actually the second person to find out about his desire to pursue marriage. After an extended time of getting to know her and praying, Jason felt confident enough to move forward. But before he went into action, he chose to give proper honor to Shelly's parents, first by asking their permission to grow closer to their daughter for the purpose of pursuing marriage.

Personally, I intend to do the same thing. In my mind, this is the best way to start off your relationship with your potential in-laws. I know this won't always be possible. Some guys I know have asked the girl first and then have gone to her parents. In other situations, a father or mother isn't close by or active in this aspect of parenthood. Whatever the case, the principle is important: A young man ought to show respect for the person responsible for the girl. If that means approaching her pastor or grandfather, do it. If it means writing, calling, or e-mailing her folks on the other side of the world, do that. Go the distance to give them the respect they deserve.

PUT YOURSELF ON TRIAL.

At this point, invite the girl's parents to ask pointed questions. What kind of plan do you have to support their daughter? What kinds of activities will you pursue as you attempt to win her hand in marriage? Parents' questions will vary depending on their relationship with their daughter and their personal convictions. Unfortunately, many parents won't really care. They may think you're being melodramatic or taking things too seriously. "Hey, if you want to take out our daughter, go for it." But many will be excited to participate in advising and counseling you during this exciting stage of the relationship.

A girl's parents may have specific concerns about the relationship or the timing of the relationship. One father I know questioned the spiritual maturity of a young man who was interested in his daughter. This young man had only recently come back to the Lord and had broken off an engagement with another girl four months earlier. The dad asked the young man to back off and prove himself over the next few months. The young guy proved himself, but not in the right way. He refused to honor the father's request and kept trying to see the girl behind her parents' backs. Finally, the girl told him that she wasn't interested in pursuing a deeper relationship with him.

No matter what response you receive from the girl's parents, be humble enough to listen and honor them. God will bless you for doing so. Remember, they've invested a big part of their lives in their daughter. And God has placed them in her life to protect her. Don't try to circumvent their authority. Instead, work with it and benefit from their wisdom.

TEST AND BUILD THE RELATIONSHIP IN REAL-LIFE SETTINGS.

Now the relationship moves into a very exciting stage that's been lost in our current pattern for relationships. Courtship is the time for the young man to win the girl's heart and for the two of them to test the wisdom of their potential marriage. It's a time of growing intimacy, but unlike the intimacy in many dating relationships, this intimacy has a purpose.

As I said before, courtship isn't a set of rules. It reflects our need today for a transitional stage between deepening friendship and engagement—a period of "principled romance." This is not a relationship simply for the sake of having romantic fun. Principled romance is purposeful in its pursuit of marriage, protected in its avoidance of sexual temptation, and accountable to parents or other Christians.

This time has distinct objectives and responsibilities. During the heart-winning/testing stage of their relationship, my friends Jeff and Danielle Myers looked for activities that allowed them to serve others and learn together. Though they did some things alone as a couple, they spent the majority of their time together with family and friends. They'd go on double dates with their parents and cook dinner for different married couples in the church.

BRINGING ROMANCE HOME.

During the season of courtship, I think going out on dates can be a healthy and important part of getting to know one another. Getting time to focus on each other isn't bad. But one of the most unfortunate aspects of contemporary dating is the way it has removed the process of romance from the warmth and reality of the home. So much of dating separates two people from the people who know and love them best instead of fusing their two families together. Later in marriage a couple will value the support and involvement of both sides of the family. Now is the time to strengthen those relationships.

Parents' support and guidance during this time, when available, is invaluable. One family wrote the following guidelines to help their daughter and her suitor. Although these guidelines were written for a specific couple with specific circumstances, I think you'll find them helpful in clarifying the purpose and focus of this stage.

1. Winston is to build Melody's trust.
2. Begin building an intimate relationship. Talk about many subjects. Discuss feelings, concerns, visions, hopes, dreams. Learn each other's basic convictions.
3. Attempt to understand each other: the differences between men and women, goals and roles, how each other thinks and responds to life.
4. Attempt to understand what things each values and detests.
5. Begin investing in each other by praying for each other, serving each other, gifting each other. Examples: Letters, phone calls, flowers.
6. Spend time together mostly in the family circle but also in short alone times—walks together, sitting in the swing together. Please avoid a "dating mentality." This is a learning and communicating time.

Even if you don't have the involvement of your parents, these kinds of guidelines can help you pursue a principled relationship.

These guidelines wisely allow love to unfold and protect the process by keeping interaction within safe boundaries. Find creative ways in your own relationship to keep the focus on learning, testing, and growth, not just on reveling in romantic love. This will allow you to truly get to know each other and make the wisest possible choice concerning marriage.

4. ENGAGEMENT.

The period of testing and winning the heart need last only as long as it takes for both people to feel confident about getting married. The time comes when observing, praying, thinking, and talking is over. Then it's time to "pop the question," as they say. By this time, a proposal should come as no surprise, yet it's still a moment to make special.

Obviously if problems and concerns arise regarding the wisdom of the union during the stage of testing, you should halt the relationship's progress or even consider calling it off. But if both of you are confident of your love for each other, and both sets of parents support your relationship, you have no reason to delay getting engaged and planning your wedding.

RESERVE PASSION FOR MARRIAGE.

Finally, throughout your God-honoring relationship, set clear guidelines for physical affection. Here I can only reiterate what we discussed in chapter 7: Purity is a direction, not a line we suddenly cross by "going too far." The enemy of your soul would love to mar the beauty of your blossoming love by leading you down a path of lust and sexual compromise. Please don't give him a foothold.

I like Elisabeth Elliot's advice to couples: "Keep your hands off and your clothes on." Until you're married, please don't treat each other as if your bodies belong to each other even if you're engaged. The kissing, touching, and caressing that take place in today's dating relationships often lead to confusion and compromise. Such behavior is often based on selfishness and awakens desires that you can righteously satisfy only in marriage. Protect each other and reserve your passion for marriage by refusing to start the process.

Personally, I've committed to waiting, even for a kiss, until I'm married. I want the first kiss with my wife to be on our wedding day. I know that sounds archaic to many, and truthfully, I would have scoffed at the idea myself four years ago. But I've come to realize how sinful and meaningless physical intimacy can be apart from the commitment and purity of marriage.

I agree with Bethany Torode (formerly Bethany Patchin), who wrote in an article entitled "(Don't) Kiss Me," "God asks different things of different people. My point is not that everyone should take a vow against premarital kissing. My challenge is that this generation of Christians would take a deeper look at something we treat so lightly. That we would take the initiative in saving something so precious for the right time and person—that we would pray about grasping what Solomon meant when he said there is a time to embrace and a time to refrain from embracing."

FOCUS ON THE SOUL.

Holding off the physical side of the relationship, though difficult, will enable you to focus on the soul of your spouse-to-be. A couple once told me their motto was, "Where physical progression begins, depth progression ends." In other words, as soon as they began to focus on the physical side of their relationship, the spiritual and emotional side ceased to deepen.

Make a commitment to God, parents, Christian mentors, friends, and your partner to let your passion sleep, storing up your desire for the marriage bed. It will awaken with joy at the proper time.

Part of keeping this kind of commitment involves avoiding settings given to temptation. This doesn't mean you can never have privacy. But two people can have privacy and time alone without completely isolating themselves from parents and friends. When you do have activities that involve just the two of you, make sure you carefully plan your time, avoid a sensual focus and atmosphere, and let someone know where you'll be and when you'll be home.

Remember, by delaying sexual involvement, you're storing up passion and making sexual love within your marriage that much more meaningful. Don't allow impatience now to rob you of an undefiled, passionate sexual relationship in marriage.

Guided by the Holy Spirit

The new pattern we've discussed is only an outline. As with anything, a couple can manipulate it to fulfill only the minimum requirements. But I believe such manipulation will rob a couple of experiencing God's best. "But when the Holy Spirit controls our lives," the Bible tells us, "he will produce this kind of fruit in us: love, joy, peace, patience, kindness, goodness, faithfulness, gentleness, and self-control" (Galatians 5:22–23, NLT). When the Holy Spirit guides our journey toward marriage, our relationships will exhibit the same qualities.

The progression from *casual friendship* to *deeper friendship* to *courtship* to *engagement* won't solve the world's relational problems. (As long as sinners like you and me are involved, we can always find a way to mess things up!) But it can move us toward a safer, wiser approach to marriage. And for those truly committed to pleasing God and loving others sincerely, I hope this new pattern can bring a much needed renewal of purity, boldness, and true romance to modern love stories. I encourage you to create your own one-of-a-kind love story by following God-honoring principles for relationships. You'll never regret seeking His best for you and your mate-to-be!

CHAPTER SIXTEEN

Someday I'll Have a Story to Tell

Writing a Love Story You'll Feel Proud to Tell

NOTHING IS QUITE as romantic as hearing an honest, unabridged account of a married couple's love story. And you are quite privileged when you can hear this story from your parents.

I grew up hearing how my parents met and married. Polaroids from family photo albums serve as visual aids to help me "see" Mom and Dad as they were when they caught each other's eye. In my mind, I step back through time, silently observing their moment of destiny...

Dayton, Ohio, is an unlikely setting for a stirring romance. Dad likes to point out that Dayton was the birthplace of both the airplane and the self-starting car engine—devices, he jokes, to help you get out of town fast. But despite my father's humorous sentiments, in 1973 this town served as the stage for my parents' love story.

As I "time travel" to 1973, I decide to visit the church my parents both attend. First Baptist Church sits on the corner of Maple and Ridgeway Street, a mix of old tradition and the young, sometimes unruly group of "Jesus people" of which my parents are a part. I find a seat at the coffeehouse located in the basement of an old house next to the church. "The Rock," as they call it, is full of high school and college students. A young man in faded jeans and a T-shirt sits on a stool in the corner of the room, playing guitar and singing. He's my father.

His hair is long and scraggly. I can't help but smile at how skinny he is. Of course he has his mustache. *Some things never change,* I think to myself.

The song he sings is simple but passionate. "Three chords and the truth," he'll call it some day in the future. I've heard this song before but by an older man who sang it for the sake of nostalgia, frequently breaking to ask, "Now how did that line go?" Here, played by someone my age, it grips me.

> *Time's coming, and it won't be long.*
> *Everybody's going to be gone.*
> *We're going to meet at the Great White Throne;*
> *Some are going to wonder what's going on.*

I had forgotten that as a young man my dad faced an unknown and confusing world, too. At this point in his life, he has only recently returned to the Lord and to his home-town of Dayton. For the last several years, he has moved from resort to resort—Laguna Beach, Lake Tahoe, Vail—playing his guitar and singing for tips in restaurants. Now the one-time hitchhiking runaway plays his guitar for Jesus. Many wonder if he'll ever amount to anything. (He will.)

My mom is here tonight, too. What a strange thing to see my mother as a beautiful young girl. I can't take my eyes off her. She has all the mannerisms as a young woman that I've observed in her throughout my life. She's so different and yet so much the same. Is it any wonder Dad grew to love her? I see her give my dad a quick glance while he plays. She's trying not to seem too impressed.

At this point in her life, Mom has been a Christian for only a year. She's still a bit headstrong and independent. At nineteen, she's a talented ballet dancer whose conversion to Christ has disrupted her ambitions for a professional career. Uncertain of her future, she's leaning toward the possibility of foreign missions. Of some things she is sure: She never wants to marry, and she never, ever wants to have children. I wonder how she'd respond if I introduced myself to her as the first of her six kids.

I steal closer to her table when I notice my dad walking over. I don't want to miss their conversation. Dad tries to appear aimless as he wanders in her direction, but he obviously wants to talk to her.

"He never was very subtle," I say quietly. I'm near enough to hear as he approaches and greets her.

"Hey, Sono, I was wondering if you and your sister need a ride home."

So this is the night! I think. I've heard the story of this conversation countless times. I lean forward to hear my mom's reply.

"No, thanks," she says. "Newton Tucker is driving us home."

My mom can be curt when she wants to, and tonight she's in full form. Completely unconcerned, she barely attempts to be polite.

"Well...maybe I can give you a call sometime," my dad says.

Thank goodness he's so clueless, I think to myself. *Any other guy would take a hint and give up. But not Dad. No siree! And it's a good thing, too. If it weren't for that indomitable Harris spirit, I wouldn't be here!*

My mom looks up at him again and gives a noncommittal "Mm-hmm," obviously inconvenienced.

206 co Joshua Harris

"Uh, what's your phone number?" he asks as she stands up to go.

She looks at him, pauses momentarily, then says, "It's in the church directory."

"Ouch!" I say out loud. "Mom can be so cold. 'It's in the directory.' Now *that* is harsh."

My dad stands silently as she walks away, and he sighs as she disappears up the steps. The situation looks pretty hopeless.

But then, I know the end of the story, and it's my favorite part. This is where God gets involved.

That night, after the infamous "It's in the directory" speech, my mom and dad prayed about each other in the privacy of their two bedrooms.

My mom's iciness toward the guitar-playing boy at the coffeehouse was not without explanation. She enjoyed his music, and his seriousness about the Lord had caught her attention. But since coming to the Lord, she had been hounded by girl-crazy Christian guys whose faith hadn't done much to rein in their hormones. More than one had told her that God had spoken to him and said she would marry him. My mom quickly learned that many guys would use religious overtures just to get the girl. She was fed up and disgusted. *Lord,* she prayed, *if this guy is different from all the rest, if he really listens to You, than tell him not to call me.* She turned off her bedroom light and went to sleep.

On the other side of town, my dad said his own prayer. A fair share of false starts with girls had left him unsure of what he should do. *God, please show me if I should call this girl.* The prayer was more a matter of form than an actual request; God had never before intervened in his romantic interests, and Dad didn't expect Him to do so this time, either. In fact, he was already planning to call and was even forming a speech that he hoped would sweep Mom off her feet.

But that night Dad encountered something different. He clearly sensed God speaking to him. "Gregg, don't call her."

God had spoken. My dad obeyed.

The rest, as they say, is history.

Confusing and Messy

Though it's hard to imagine, someday I'll tell my children the story I'm writing with my life today. But that realization does little to save me from the puzzling maze called now. "History never looks like history when you're living through it," says John Gardner. "It always looks confusing and messy, and it always feels uncomfortable."

As I stand on this side of matrimony with no potential mate in sight, I'm right in the middle of the messiness and confusion. I still have so many questions. Will I know when I'm walking through my story for the first time? Will I recognize the event that will begin the chapters of my love story with my mate? Will time stand still for one moment to tell me that this person—this one person, out of all the billions bustling on the planet—is *the one*? Will I realize when it happens? Or might I miss it?

Some questions are probably best left unasked. I know I should push them aside and wait for life to unfold its mysteries. Someday when I'm older and wiser I'll sit back and tell my story to someone who will listen. And as I tell my story, will I remember the doubts and questioning prayers of today? Or will I have forgotten the silent longings; will they wash away like footprints on an ocean shore? I'll probably tell some young fool the same things I get so tired of hearing from others. I'll tell him to bide his time, "for it's sure to work out in the end." And of course, "you can't rush these things."

Someday I'll have a story to tell. So will you. How will you respond when one day you look back on your love story? Will it bring tears of joy or tears of remorse? Will it remind you of God's goodness or your lack of faith in that goodness? Will it be a story of purity, faith, and selfless love? Or will it be a story of impatience, self-ishness, and compromise? It's your choice.

I encourage you (and continue to remind myself) to write a love story with your life that you'll feel proud to tell.

Boy Meets Girl

THE CLOCK READ 5:05 P.M. Shannon's workday was over. She enjoyed her job at the church, but she was ready to go home and unwind.

She began her familiar end-of-the-day routine: tidied her desk, shut down her computer, straightened a picture on her bookshelf, got her coat from the closet, and said her goodbyes. "Bye, Nicole," she said to the girl in the office beside her. "See you tomorrow, Helen," she called to the receptionist.

She walked through the quiet lobby and pushed open one of the heavy glass doors. The winter wind tugged at her as she made her way across the nearly empty parking lot. She climbed into her worn, navy blue Honda Accord and shut out the cold.

She lifted her keys to the ignition, and then paused. There, alone in the silence, the emotions she had kept at bay during the day came rushing in. Tears welled up in her eyes. She leaned her forehead against the steering wheel and began to cry.

"Why, Lord?" she whispered. "Why is this so hard? What am I supposed to do with these feelings? Take them away if they're not from You."

I used to watch from my window as Shannon walked to her car at the end of each day. My office looked out over the parking lot. *What is she thinking about?* I wondered. I longed to know more about her—to go beyond our polite conversations as casual friends and coworkers and really get to know her.

But was it the right time? My heart had been wrong so many times before. Could I trust my feelings? Would she return my interest?

From my vantage point, Shannon Hendrickson seemed happy, confident, and oblivious of me. I was sure she liked another guy. As I watched her drive away, I whispered my own prayer. *What is Your will, God? Is she the one? Help me to be patient. Show me when to act. Help me trust You.*

How could I know that the girl in the navy blue Honda was crying as she drove away, or that I was the cause of her tears?

Three Months Later...

I was twenty-three years old, but my hands were acting like they'd never dialed a phone number. I gripped my cordless phone as if it were a wild animal trying to escape and tried again.

You can do this, I assured myself.

The phone rang three times before an answering machine picked up. She wasn't home. I gritted my teeth. *Should I leave a message?* The machine beeped, and I took the plunge.

"Hey, Shannon, this is Josh...uh, Harris."

I was sure my voice made it obvious how nervous I felt. I'd never called her at home before, and I had no excuse related to work or church for doing so now. "Um...could you give me a call when you get a chance? Thanks." I hung up, feeling like a complete idiot.

For sixty-four agonizing minutes I analyzed whether or not the message I had left sounded cool and collected. Then the phone rang. I took a deep breath and answered.

It was Shannon.

"Hey, thanks for calling me back. How's it going?"

We chatted for a few minutes about her day and did our best to have a natural conversation, even though we both knew that my calling her was the most unnatural thing in the world. I finally got to the point and asked if she could meet me the next day after work at Einstein's, a local bagel shop. She said she could.

Before we hung up, I offered an ambiguous explanation for the rendezvous. "I need to talk…about a guy I know who's interested in you."

Good Questions

My phone call to Shannon might not seem like a big deal to most people, but for me it was monumental.

Why? Because five years earlier I had quit dating. I know that sounds strange, so let me explain. I had come to believe that the lifestyle of short-term relationships was a detour from serving God as a single. So while I kept my social life, my female friends, and my desire to get married someday, I stopped dating.

This new perspective was anything but characteristic of me. I had always been a flirt who lived for the buzz of romance. For me, rejecting the dating game was a seismic shift.

My change of perspective began after I broke up with a girl I'd been going out with for two years. Our relationship was an area of my life that I had refused to submit to God. When it ended, He began to show me just how selfish I was. I'd used her to satisfy my own sinful desires. Even though we never went all the way, I had led her into a sinful physical relationship. I had hurt her. I had broken a lot of promises.

For the first time, I really began to question how my faith as a

Christian affected my love life. There had to be more to it than "don't have sex" and "only date Christians." What did it mean to truly love a girl? What did it feel like to really be pure—in my body *and* my heart? And how did God want me to spend my single years? Was it merely a time to try out different girls romantically?

Slowly and in spite of my resistance, God peeled away layer after layer of wrong thinking, wrong values, and wrong desires. He changed my heart. And as my heart changed, I saw that my lifestyle had to change, too.

When I was twenty-one, I wrote about my experience in *I Kissed Dating Goodbye*. I wanted to challenge other singles to reconsider the way they pursued a romance in light of God's Word. "If we aren't really ready for commitment, what's the point of getting into intimate and romantic relationships?" I asked. "Why not enjoy friendship with the opposite sex but use our energy as singles to serve God?"

To my astonishment God provided a publisher willing to print my oddly titled book. To everyone's astonishment the book actually sold. It turned out that many people besides me were rethinking romance. I have received thousands of e-mails, postcards, and letters from singles of all ages from all over the world who want to share their stories, ask questions, and get advice.

As the letters poured in, I realized that while God had graciously used my book to help some people, it had also raised a lot of questions.

For example, if you don't date, how exactly do you end up married? One girl wrote: "I want to avoid the pitfalls of our culture's approach to romance, but how do I get close enough to a guy to decide whether I want to marry him? What comes between friendship and marriage?"

The main point of *I Kissed Dating Goodbye* was: "If you're not ready for marriage, *wait* on romance." But now my fellow singles were asking, "How can you know when you *are* ready for marriage? And once you're ready, what should you do?"

To be honest, I hadn't figured that out yet. I never meant to become an expert on relationships. The questions my readers were asking were the same ones weighing on my heart.

This is why my phone call to Shannon was such a big deal. I'd reached a point where I felt ready to pursue marriage, and I was deeply attracted to her. What now? For five years I'd experienced God's faithfulness as I *waited* on romance; now I was stepping into the unknown believing that He would continue to be faithful as I *pursued* romance.

The guy who had "kissed dating goodbye" was about to "say hello to courtship."

Read the Rest of the Story

We hope you've enjoyed this brief "preview" of Josh's second book, *Boy Meets Girl*. This bestselling follow-up to *I Kissed Dating Goodbye* focuses on the season of courtship. It's a book for people who are ready to pursue a serious relationship and want to do so in a way that honors God.

Boy Meets Girl is an invaluable guide on the journey from friendship to engagement. In it you'll find helpful topics like:

- How to know if you're ready to move beyond friendship into courtship
- How to grow close to each other yet still guard your heart
- What to do with your lips: practical advice on clear communication
- Resisting sexual temptation when you're in love
- Working through the pain of past sexual sin and experiencing God's forgiveness
- Ten essential questions to ask *before* you get engaged

If you're single, *Boy Meets Girl* will give you a clear vision of the kind of relationship God wants you to wait for. If you're in a relationship, *Boy Meets Girl* is the perfect book to read as a couple. Here's what readers are saying:

Boy Meets Girl was a *huge* encouragement to my Christian growth. The book made me excited for my love story some-day, and it challenged me to live as a godly single and start building the character I need for marriage. You said your hope for *Boy Meets Girl* was that it would make the reader more passionate about God. Well, Josh, God used your book to do exactly that. Thanks so much for the challenging and encouraging message. —Jesse

After reading your first book I found out that you had writ-ten a sequel. I went out as soon as possible and bought it. It was such a help to me! It helped me see the difference between dating and courtship. I know that God is preparing me for the future with the help of your books. Most impor-tantly I want to thank Shannon. I, too, lost my virginity at a young age. Now at the age of thirty-two I look back at the times I've given myself to men and I think about the day when I'll have to do as Shannon did and have that serious talk with the man who's courting me. It helped to read your book. —Lisa

If you enjoyed *I Kissed Dating Goodbye,* take the next step and get *Boy Meets Girl.*

Not Even a Hint: Guarding Your Heart Against Lust

by Joshua Harris

I KNOW YOU WANT to be free from the hurt and consequences of lust. You desire the joy and freedom found in living a life of holiness that pleases God. But how can you be victorious when lust is everywhere?

Images that provoke lust ooze from magazine pages and jump off television and movie screens. Problems with lust are rampant throughout society today, yet much of the world doesn't see anything wrong with it and even promotes it as good.

But lust *is* a problem. And God hates it. So should you.

My next book, *Not Even a Hint,* is about hating lust and loving holiness—about understanding the soul-destroying danger of lust and impurity and the joy and freedom of loving God and living in holiness.

Written for men and women in this generation, *Not Even a Hint* is straightforward about sexual sin without being graphic. It's written for a broad audience—for a generation that is willing to challenge conventions. It's a call for people to turn to God's standards for their lives. I expose the tactics of lust in the human heart and how to create a personal and practical plan for fighting back. We'll look at:

- How to recognize that you have a problem
- How to learn the enemy's strategy—and fight back
- How to sign up with God's plan for lasting change

To be honest, I'm scared to take on this topic. I've struggled with lust throughout my life. Speaking out about something so many people battle alone in silence isn't easy. But I believe God wants me to write about how *His grace can rescue us* from the lies of lust.

I want you to know about the life-transformation God makes available through faith in Jesus Christ. And I think this book will bless you. So pick up a copy. It's available in stores September 2003.

But among you there must not be even a hint of sexual immorality. (Ephesians 5:3, NIV)

Thanks,
Joshua Harris

Thanks...

To Apple computers for the PowerBook G3.

To all the people who helped make the first edition of this book possible. In particular, Randy Alcorn and Stephanie Storey, who got my foot in the door at Multnomah. I'll never forget being an unpublished author hoping someone would give me a chance. Thank you, Don Jacobson, for taking a risk on a first-time author.

To my mom and dad, who were, and always will be, my first editors. Thank you for nursing me through writer's block and rejoicing with me over every finished chapter. My triumph is your triumph. My victory is yours. I love you.

And for those who helped to make this "upgrade" a reality.

To Sam Torode, for the foreword.

To C. J. Mahaney for all your feedback on the content of the book and for teaching me to be a pastor.

To Corby Megorden, whose diligent work allowed me to write.

To Jennifer Gott, my editor, who taught me how to use tracking in Word. Thanks for all your help.

To Nicole Whitacre, who went through the first edition and gave me so many excellent suggestions about how to make it better.

To Doug Gabbert, whose vision to do a new edition and encouragement along the way was essential to this project.

To Kevin Marks, who has always encouraged me to write what God has put on my heart. Thanks for being a faithful friend all these years.

To Shannon. God knew as I wrote each word of this book that He had you waiting for me. That's awesome!

And finally, and most importantly, to Jesus Christ. I'm grateful to say I know You better than I did five years ago. I'm more amazed by Your mercy and more in awe of Your power. Thank You for saving me.

About the Author

Joshua Harris got his start in writing as the editor of *New Attitude,* a Christian magazine for homeschool teens. He wrote *I Kissed Dating Goodbye* at age twenty-one and that same year moved from Oregon to Gaithersburg, Maryland, to be trained for pastoral ministry under C. J. Mahaney at Covenant Life Church. Five years after giving up the dating game himself, he met, courted, and married his new bride, Shannon. He shares their love story and the lessons God taught them in his second book, *Boy Meets Girl: Say Hello to Courtship.*

Joshua and Shannon now have two children, Emma and Joshua Quinn. Josh serves as the executive pastor at Covenant Life. He also hosts an annual conference for college students and singles each January called "New Attitude." He's currently working on *Not Even a Hint,* a book about hating lust and loving holiness, due out fall 2003. For information about Josh's work, visit his website at:

www.joshharris.com

Feel free to contact Josh. Though he can't respond personally to all correspondence, he'd love to get your feedback.

Joshua Harris
P.O. Box 249
Gaithersburg, MD 20884-0249
DOIT4JESUS@aol.com

Notes

CHAPTER 2

Wendy Shalit—Wendy Shalit, *A Return to Modesty* (New York: Free Press, 1999).

Stephen Olford—Stephen Olford, "Social Relationships," a sermon recorded at Moody Bible Institute.

CHAPTER 3

C. S. Lewis—C. S. Lewis, *The Four Loves* (Orlando, Fla.: Harcourt Brace and Company, 1960), 66.

Elisabeth Elliot—Elisabeth Elliot, *Passion and Purity* (Grand Rapids, Mich.: Baker Book House, 1984), 153.

CHAPTER 6

William J. Bennett—William J. Bennett, *The Book of Virtues* (New York: Simon and Schuster, 1993), 57.

Marshmallows—Nancy Gibbs, "The EQ Factor," *Time* (2 October 1995), 60.

Elisabeth Elliot—Elisabeth Elliot, *Passion and Purity,* 164.

John Fischer—John Fischer, "A Single Person's Identity," a sermon delivered August 5, 1973, at Peninsula Bible Church, Palo Alto, Calif.

May Riley Smith—May Riley Smith, "Sometime," *The Best Loved Poems of the American People* (New York: Doubleday and Company, 1936), 299.

CHAPTER 7

"Recognize the Deep Significance of Physical Intimacy"—I am indebted to Lynn Denby, who wrote me a letter and challenged my thinking about how guys and girls should relate before marriage.

Billy Graham—William Martin, *A Prophet with Honor: The Billy Graham Story* (New York: William Morrow and Company, 1991), 107.

CHAPTER 10

Elisabeth Elliot—Elisabeth Elliot, *The Mark of a Man* (Grand Rapids, Mich.: Fleming H. Revell), 102.

C. S. Lewis—C. S. Lewis, *The Four Loves,* 66.

CHAPTER 11

Elisabeth Elliot—Elisabeth Elliot, *Passion and Purity,* 31.

Beilby Porteus—Dr. Ruth C. Haycock, ed. *The Encyclopedia of Bible Truths for School Subjects* (Association of Christian Schools, 1993), 393.

CHAPTER 12

Catherine Vos—Catherine F. Vos, *The Child's Story Bible* (Grand Rapids, Mich.: William B. Eerdmans Publishing Company), 29. Used with permission.

Gregg Harris—Gregg Harris, "The Adventure of Current Obligations," *The Family Restoration Quarterly* 1 (February 1987), 2.

CHAPTER 13

Ricucci—Gary Ricucci and Betsy Ricucci, *Love that Lasts: Making a Magnificent Marriage* (Gaithersburg, Md.: People of Destiny, 1992), 7–10. Used with permission.

Ann Landers—Ann Landers, "All Marriages Are Happy." Permission granted by Ann Landers and Creators Syndicate.

Lena Lathrop—Lena Lathrop, "A Woman's Question," *The Best Loved Poems of the American People* (New York: Doubleday and Company, 1936), 22.

CHAPTER 14

Randy Alcorn—Randy Alcorn, "O. J. Simpson: What Can We Learn?" *Eternal Perspectives* (Summer 1994).

William Davis—William Davis, "Reputation and Character," *The Treasure Chest: Memorable Words of Wisdom and Inspiration* (San Francisco: Harper Collins, 1995), 54.

Samuel Smiles—William Thayer, *Gaining Favor with God and Man* (San Antonio: Mantle Ministries, 1989), 41.

David Powlison and John Yenchko—David Powlison and John Yenchko, "Should We Get Married?" *Journal of Biblical Counseling* 14, (Spring 1996), 42.

A. W. Tozer—A. W. Tozer, *The Best of A. W. Tozer* (Grand Rapids, Mich.: Baker Book House, 1978), 111.

Charlotte Mason—Charlotte M. Mason, *The Original Homeschooling Series* 1 (Wheaton, Ill.: Tyndale House Publishers, 1989).

Bill Bennett—William J. Bennett, *The Book of Virtues,* 347.

E. V. Hill—James Dobson, *Focus on the Family Newsletter* (February 1995), 3.

Benjamin Tillett—*The Encyclopedia of Religious Quotations* (Westwood, N.J.: Fleming H. Revell Co., 1965), 298.

Benjamin Franklin—*Notable Quotables* (Chicago: World Book Encyclopedia, 1984), 65.

CHAPTER 15

Wycliffe—Charles F. Pfeiffer, ed. *Wycliffe Bible Commentary* (Chicago: Moody Press, 1962), 603.

"Guidelines for Winston and Melody"—Kenneth and Julie McKim, *Family Heritage Newsletter* (September 1994).

"(Don't) Kiss Me"—Bethany Patchin, "(Don't) Kiss Me," *Boundless webzine* www.boundless.org/2000/departments/beyond_buddies/a000016. html. (accessed 12 November 2002).

Elisabeth Elliot—Elisabeth Elliot, *Quest for Love* (Grand Rapids, Mich.: Baker Book House, 1996), 269.

CHAPTER 16

Dad's Song—Gregg Harris, "It's a Shame," © 1972.

John Gardner—*Notable Quotables*, 48.

LUST TELLS YOU LIES.
THE TRUTH SETS YOU FREE.

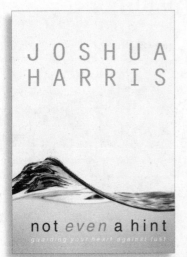

I wrote this book for both men and women. Why? Because lust isn't a male problem. It's a human problem. Lust ruins our relationships, robs us of spiritual passion, and leaves us feeling hollow...

But the truth is that you and I don't have to stay on that treadmill of guilt and shame. God calls us to a high standard—not even a hint of sexual impurity. And He gives us everything we need to make it a reality.

If you're ready for a practical, grace-centered plan for defeating lust and celebrating purity, I hope you'll join me on a most promising journey.

—Joshua Harris

ISBN 1-59052-147-1

BOY MEETS GIRL. NOW WHAT?

I Kissed Dating Goodbye shocked the publishing world in 1995 with its metoric rise to the top of bestseller lists. Teens wanted more than dating "rules"—they wanted an intentional, God-pleasing game plan. In this dynamic sequel, newlyweds Joshua and Shannon Harris deliver an inspiring and practical illustration of how this healthy, joyous alternative to recreational dating—biblical courtship—worked for them.

Boy Meets Girl helps readers understand how to go about pursuing the possibility of marriage with someone they may be serious about. It's the natural follow-up to the author's blockbuster book on teen dating!

ISBN 1-57673-709-8

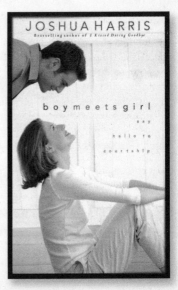

I KISSED DATING GOODBYE
VIDEO SERIES

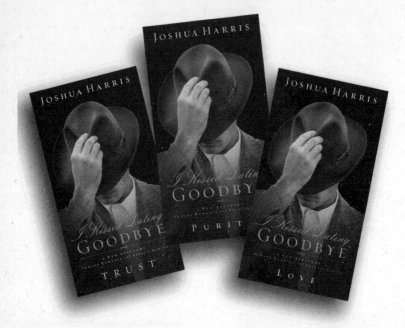

The Searching for True Love video series by Joshua Harris builds on his highly popular conference series and bestselling book *I Kissed Dating Goodbye* to give young adults God's direction as they seek a lifetime love. Available in a three-pack or separately, the videos explore love, purity, and trust from the Bible's perspective. They also help young adults answer vital questions like "How can I honor God in my love life?" and "Is it possible to practice purity in today's society?" Forty-five minutes each.

Three-video series	ISBN 1-59052-180-3
I Kissed Dating Goodbye Video-Part 1: Love	ISBN 1-59052-212-5
I Kissed Dating Goodbye Video-Part 1: Purity	ISBN 1-59052-213-3
I Kissed Dating Goodbye Video-Part 1: Trust	ISBN 1-59052-214-1